King of the Black Isles

J. U. NICOLSON

Ether Editors

Ether Editions

Contents

FOREWORD   1

PART ONE   5

TO ----------   7

IF   8

TO COLUMBINE   9

FAITH AND I'M IN LOVE AGAIN   10

FUTILITY OF SINGING   11

TO A PRETTY WOMAN   12

A LOVE SONG   13

TO A MAIDEN SINGING   15

NEED YOU KNOW?   16

SHALL SOMEONE SING?   17

AFTERWARDS   19

STRING STARS FOR PEARLS   20

CHANSONETTE D'AMOUR   21

THERE WILL BE THIS   22

MONODY   23

FROM HAUNTED HALLS   24

CHANSON DE MYSTERE   25

DEGRADATION   26

LOVE IS A THIEF   27

TO ONE IN APRIL WEATHER   28

I SAID I WOULD NOT BIND ME   29

SONG TO BE SAID AT DAYBREAK   30

TO LEAVE IN MAY   31

EXILE   32

IF I REMEMBER   33

PIQUE   34

RECONCILIATION   35

PART TWO   37

MOUNTEBANK   39

YET AGAIN AND YET AGAIN   40

ROMANCE   42

WAY OF A MAID WITH A MAN   43

FOR LOVE IS OF THE VALLEY   44

A CHRISTMAS IDYLL   45

AND ONE WITH SECRET TEARS   47

RENUNCIATION   48

MOOD   49

I WOULD REMEMBER CONSTANT THINGS   50

A LAMENT   52

THE KINGS THAT FOUGHT FOR HELEN   53

ONE DAY   54

SONG FOR THE SAKE OF SINGING   56

SONG BEFORE DYING   58

RUSTIC   60

SAILOR SONG   62

CITY BRED   64

WHALER'S CHANTEY   66

A WANDER SONG   68

OLD SHIPS   70

MELODY   72

WILD   73

OF MIST AND AIR   74

BLIND   76

A LADY LIVED IN LESBOS   78

THE STREETS OF HELL   79

IN PASSING   80

IN BABYLON, IN BABYLON   82

THEN COMETH ATROPOS   84

A DRINKING SONG   86

I'LL RUN NO MORE   87

DESERTED   88

PROPHECY   89

PART THREE   91

THE KING OF THE BLACK ISLES   93

BEFORE DAWN   99

BEAUTY   110

THE STREETS BEYOND BAGDAD   116

JUDITH   123

BATHSHEBA   141

MICHAL   148

ABISHAG   153

A SONG OF SOLOMON   159

THE WANDERER   161

BLACK MARGOT   164

DAUGHTERS OF JOY   166

DISAVOWAL   169

PART FOUR   175

BALLADE TO THE PURITANS   177

BALLADE OF MUTABILITY   179

BALLADE OF TWO LADIES   181

BALLADE OF MAN'S LAST NEED   183

BALLADE IN TIME OF THE GREAT WAR   185

PARIS — 1456   187

BALLADE OF LADIES OF TIMES GONE BY   189

BALLADE OF LOST ILLUSION   191

BALLADE TO A LADY IN IDLENESS   193

BALLADE OF ROMANCE DESIRED   195

RONDEL   197

RONDEAU OF REST   198

SESTINA OF ONE FACE FAIR   199

SESTINA TO A LADY OF STERN VIRTUE   201

RIME-ROYAL OF HIS OWN SINGING   203

RIME-ROYAL OF BETTER COUNSEL THAN MOST   205

HENDECASYLLABICS   207

SAPPHICS I   208

SAPPHICS II   210

ALCAICS   212

PART FIVE   213

SONNETS OF A MINNESINGER   215

NAPOLEON   238

TO A POET DYING YOUNG   239

VIKINGS   240

BORGIA   241

IN MEMORIAM   242

OLD MAID   243

THE JEST   244

TO OMAR KHAYYAM   245

CONRAD   246

BOSWORTH FIELD   247

ACROSTIC   248

J. U. Nicolson   251

KING OF THE BLACK ISLES

FOREWORD

J. U. Nicolson was a twentieth-century American poet and translator of poetry. Born John Urban Nicolson on October 9th, 1885, in Alma, Kansas, he spent most of his professional life in Chicago, where he served as General Manager of the Central Storage & Forwarding Company.

Nicolson first achieved notice as a "column poet," so-called for the appearance of his early work in the literary columns of several Chicago newspapers under the pseudonym, "The King of the Black Isles." The popular response to his poems soon brought Nicolson to the attention of local publishers Pascal Covici and William McGee. Their fledgling firm, Covici-McGee, brought out Nicolson's first book, *King of the Black Isles*, in early 1924. In his introduction to the book, Keith Preston, then literary editor of the *Chicago Daily News*, recounted how the poetry of J. U. Nicolson was initially discovered by Chicago-area readers.

> "Some two years ago in the *Line o' Type* column of the *Chicago Tribune*, conducted by Richard Henry Little, occurred one of those sudden flurries of excitement that are the life of column conducting. There appeared a poem, "most musical, most melancholy," over the magical pseudonym "The King of the Black Isles." Response to the new voice was immediate and general. The conductor was showered with letters requesting

more verse from this poet potentate, which, in due course, was vouchsafed. Since then, "The King's" success has been confirmed, and not only in his first demesne but in other Chicago columns. In *Hit or Miss* on the *Chicago Daily News* and in *Pillar to Post* on the *Chicago Evening Post*, his poems have been waited for, welcomed, clipped, and pasted into scrapbooks. In mediums where good verse is no rarity his success has been conspicuous.

The appeal of J. U. Nicolson — behold, "The King of the Black Isles" unmasked! — is an ancient magic. Musical before anything else, his masters are the singing poets from Villon to Swinburne. His escape from our perturbed and petty present lies most often in the pomps and splendors of the past. Even in love he is not too immediate. It is the still glowing embers of passion that he prefers to contemplate wistfully, yet with no lack of warmth when all is said. In this romantic field we can think of no American poet that parallels Nicolson at this moment."

When *King of the Black Isles* appeared in the local bookstores in February 1924, *Line 'o Type* columnist Richard Henry Little ventured to speculate on the origins of the author's poetic pseudonym. "His name is J. U. Nicolson and he is the manager of a big storage warehouse on Pershing road. Storage warehouse — long, dark passageways — get it now? "The King of the Black Aisles." Nicolson, however, disabused the columnist of such a curious notion, explaining that the pseudonym was inspired by his reading of *The Arabian Nights*.

While J. U. Nicolson had his champions among newspapermen, one Chicago reviewer was less impressed. Harriet Monroe, founding editor and publisher of *Poetry* magazine, opined that Nicolson had "ransacked every treasure-chest in history or legendry for rich garments to parade in, and sounded every tune the elder bards provide to which he could manage to fit the light lilt of his measures."

King of the Black Isles was reprinted half a dozen times during its first year of publication, and its success would encourage Nicolson to produce several other books of poetry during the 1920s. *The Sainted Courtezan* with illustrations by Boris Riedel was published in a limited edition of 1,550 copies in late summer, 1924. *The Drums of Yle*, an epic romantic poem set in medieval England, appeared in an edition of 1,100 copies will illustrations by Earl H. Reed in spring, 1925. Nicolson's *Sonnets of a Minnesinger* and *The Road to Antioch*, the latter edition published by the Druid Press of Chicago, appeared the following year.

Pascal Covici brought out a revised and expanded edition of *King of the Black Isles* late in 1926. This new edition included Nicolson's meticulous revisions to the first edition as well as additional poems that were culled from his previous books. Nicolson also re-ordered the poems appearing in the 1926 edition and set them into five constituent parts, thereby making it the author's most fully realized edition of the work. This final edition of *King of the Black Isles* is republished herein.

J. U. Nicolson would go on to translate the works of two major poets of the Middle Ages. His two-volume edition of the French poet François Villon's collected works, with illustrations by Alexander King, was published by Pascal Covici in 1928. In a later review appearing in the *New York Times*, Richard Le Gallienne wrote that "Mr. Nicolson is a good poet himself, and none but a poet should translate a poet; he is evidently a sufficient scholar too, and saturated in the atmosphere and the literature of his subject."

Apart from *King of the Black Isles*, J. U. Nicolson is best remembered for his rendering into modern English of *The*

Canterbury Tales of Geoffrey Chaucer. Originally published by Pascal Covici and Donald Friede in 1934, this new edition of Chaucer included illustrations by Rockwell Kent and an introduction by the noted American folklorist and Chaucer scholar Gordon Hall Gerould. Often reprinted, Nicolson's rendering of *The Canterbury Tales* has served to introduce Chaucer to generations of readers.

J. U. Nicolson produced one novel later in his writing career, a supernatural horror story entitled *Fingers of Fear*, which met with mixed reviews upon its publication in 1937. A *Los Angeles Times* reviewer called the book "chilling, magnificently written, ending in a scene that will make you leap from your chair and yell." A reviewer for the *Washington Evening Star* gave the novel short shrift, calling it an "average good thriller."

John Urban Nicolson married Ida May Nicolson, née Platz, in 1917. The couple spent much of their last decade together in Mason, New Hampshire, where Nicolson was serving as Chairman of Mason's Board of Selectman when he died suddenly on October 27th, 1944, after suffering a heart attack. His wife Ida would survive him for over a decade. They are both buried in Prospect Hill Cemetery in Mason.

Poet J. U. Nicolson's New Hampshire death certificate lists his profession as "Manager of Warehouse."

Ether Editors

PART ONE

Goodby, and if you will, forget,
There are so many men
Another's arm will comfort you
When spring comes round again.

TO ----------

Unto the end and beyond the end!
For out of my dust a rose shall grow
And out of my heart a wind shall go
To carry the scent of the rose to you,
Till you, too, into the dust descend
To lie beside me the long night through.

IF

If I should make a song for you,
   What would you do with it?
Sing it to a new lover
   Or only sigh and sit? ...

The wind among the maple trees,
   Murmuring in your hair,
Is older than a melody
   Of any lute player.

And rain upon a quiet beach,
   Droning over the sand,
Can tell of kings in Avalon
   And queens in Samarcand. . . .

If I should make a song for you,
   What would you have me sing?
Semiramis or the crack o' dawn
   Or a posy for a ring?

TO COLUMBINE

You ask me for a song, but I
    Would rather kiss your lips again
Than sing the stars out, one by one,
    And name them, too, for men.

And I would rather kiss your throat
    And kiss your closed white eyelids up
Than have that gold by Helen's breast
    Once molded for a cup.

You ask me for a song. Ah Love,
    What bells unstruck can ever chime?
But ring me with a kiss and I
    Will break your heart with rhyme!

FAITH AND I'M IN LOVE AGAIN

Faith and I'm in love again, though none there is to
     guess it
  (Splendors on the city streets and roses in the air);
All my heart's afire again, but why should I confess it?
  What's the gain of getting back the chains I used to
     wear?

Ache of empty arms again, but I'll not let her know it
  (Books beneath the balcony and wine beneath the
     stair);
All the world's at odds again, but how am I to sow it?
  Where's the good of being caught in coils of tumbled
     hair?

Faith and I'm in love again, and I'll be gay about it
  (Friends and many plays to see and gaudy clothes to
     wear);
All my days are glad again, and I can live without it,
  But oh, the face that follows me and haunts me
     everywhere!

FUTILITY OF SINGING

In rain and wind I made a song of her,
    A little sweet sad song for ease of pain,
Full of blown gold and silver, lovelier
    Than April's dancing in the wind and rain.

I made a song of her upon the sands
    While yet the darkening west was all ablaze,
Singing her face, from many ways and lands
    Beyond the seas through many lands and ways.

And then I made a song of her, at last,
    Wherein were only tenderness and rest
And dreams long time remembered of the past
    And dusk of hair let down upon her breast.

And all my songs are music, all my songs
    Are music as of harp and dulcimer,
But I can strike no chord wherein belongs
    The melody of the mystery of her.

TO A PRETTY WOMAN

You are a bugle blown for a weary bivouac;
   You are the splendor of blood on burnished blades;
You are the west wind over a waste of sedges;
   And you are a teak-wood cabinet filled with jades.

You are a topaz burned alone in a casket;
   You are a glass to be drained and flung to the floor;
You are a reed that one might fashion for music;
   You are a woman and you are nothing more.

But in your eyes are the flames that flow in an opal;
   Your mouth is hot as a roseleaf crushed from a rose;
You are the lie and the lure of all that is beauty . . .
   And how I shall ever be quit of you now — God knows!

A LOVE SONG

I know I shall not love again
    White limbs of women langorous,
But yours will come before me, then,
    And blind me with their beauty, thus.
For eyes that wake to see the sun,
    What lamp shall light the world by day?
And for what faith, when life done,
    Shall God have power to pay?

I know there shall not wait for me
    Fond fingers and desirous lips,
But I'll remember, dangerously,
    Your mouth and fevered fingertips.
River by river down the vales
    We moved to meet the deeps of death,
And in what ocean shall the gales
    Be sweet with gardens' breath?

(cont'd., new stanza)

I know I shall not find again
    Desire of burning songs to sing
Nor any meaning more in men
    Nor hope again in any thing.
For oh, know that if my heart
    Can change before its dying day,
Then all this world can break and part
    And utterly pass away!

TO A MAIDEN SINGING

I think it, will be summer in your heart
    When you, are old;
I think you will have beauty stored apart
    And hoarded gold.
The souls that drink so deeply of the sun
    Shall never thirst as those that drink the sea.
O laughing lady, when my songs are done,
    Sing, then, for me!

In plumes and painted armory I ride
    While you go bare
With truant roses of the summertide
    Twined in your hair.
My days are full of light from burnished thrones
    And all the wonders of the world I see;
But oh, when I am only buried bones,
    Remember me!

NEED YOU KNOW?

I am come from Eastern Inds
   In a vessel flown like fire
Joyously on streaming winds
   To your arms of my desire.
I have brought you rugs and rings,
   Amber combs and gods to kiss,
Pearls and myriad painted things —
   Ask no more than this!

On your body you shall wear
   Silks and gold of Samarcand —
Silks and gold — and in your hair
   Perfumes out of Tartar-land.
I am come with arms of flame
   Where I loved in younger years —
Need you know what secret shame
   Drinks my secret tears?

SHALL SOMEONE SING?

When bright with gold Cuchulain's brand
　　Flung silver death to the breasts of men,
What braid, by strand and ruddier strand,
　　Was dyed in the red dew falling then?
What queen of a misty realm or girl
　　Of the Everliving by some lone sea
Wove her hands in a kindred curl
　　And keened in the wan wind anxiously?

Who was the woman great with love
　　That Sargon left at the Persian hills
For a gem set deep in gold whereof
　　The song of a war-king throbs and thrills?
In a chamber painted with all delight,
　　In a bower blushed with a rhythm of rose,
What princess wept alone in the night
　　And wept in the dawn alone — who knows?

(cont'd., new stanza)

17

O fair young girls blown over with dust
    And blown like dust on the desert, now,
What kings have kissed you, livid with lust,
    Having gold on breast and delicate brow?
And O my girl that I kiss tonight,
    When the world has circled a thousand years
Shall someone sing of your dead delight
    And strike from a sounding string your tears?

AFTERWARDS

When you have leashed the hawk desire
   By jess and varvel
     You will sit,
Silent, beside your daughter's fire
   And she will marvel,
     While you knit,
That one there was who loved to rhyme
   Your face with all he dreamed or said —
When you are old and tired of time
   And I am dead.

Ah, love, the days are overfleet
   Before December,
     Though we spend
Not all the summer's gold and, sweet,
   Though we remember
     Till the end.
There shall be time to chide desire
   When all our passionate prayers are said
And you are old beside the fire
   And I am dead.

STRING STARS FOR PEARLS

String stars for pearls on a ribbon of whim
    And fling it about her shoulders;
Carve cups from coral and crust each brim
    Till the whole gem smokes and smolders;
Bring gold for beating in thick bright rings
    And honey from hearts of clover;
But love will long for the absent things,
    Ever the old earth over.

Go, ride the world in a glory of wars
    And startle the Gods to wonder;
Break men to follow triumphant cars
    With a rose-paved road thereunder;
Pile stone on stone for the bruit of a name
    When a thousand years dissever;
But love will lean to a smaller flame
    Forever and forever.

CHANSONETTE
D'AMOUR

O blossoms white on apple boughs,
    And flame of love!
O burdens of bent apple boughs
    And fruits of love!
Love cometh like a border thief
Nor beareth part in any grief
And bright with all desire and brief
    The life of love.

O grapes that grow on purpled hills
    And wine of love!
O withered vines on winter's hills
    And lees of love!
Love hath his day of troubled breath
And, passing, utterly perisheth,
And bitterer than all other death
    The death of love.

THERE WILL BE THIS

There will be this between us two
    Hereafter when our love is done
And I am gone away and you
    Sit with the spinners in the sun —
There will be this, that all our days,
    Till flesh and blood have ceased to sing,
We shall not meet and go our ways
    Without remembering.

We shall not meet and go our ways
    As two that never loved may do,
For there were nights and there were days
    Known only but to me and you.
And we may sigh or we may hate,
    But oh, remember then we must,
However long the hour and late,
    However near the dust.

MONODY

The hills are painted with glory,
   The seas are heavy with sound,
And one may look on the wide sky
   The whole year round.

There is no end of beauty
   And never an end of song
And one may harbor a deep dream
   All life long.

And June comes over with roses
   And memories, one by one,
But the kiss we 'changed on a dim day —
   That is done.

FROM HAUNTED HALLS

If we should meet, my love and I,
   At our old garden gates, alone,
And see our Spanish castle lie
   A crumbling ruins, ivy-grown,
Would we go thence, my love and I,
   To some small cottage near a stream
Or — oft I ponder — would we sigh
   And part to mourn a shattered dream?

If we should meet, my love and I,
   And stand without the broken door,
Well might we fear what now must lie
   Where happiness was housed of yore.
And would we dare, my love and I,
   Cover a meaner hearth and walls
With arras of a day gone by
   And trophies torn from haunted halls?

CHANSON DE MYSTERE

They say heard melodies are sweet,
  But those unheard are sweeter far;
And two may dream and never meet
  Beneath one star.

And two may live their whole lives through,
  Wanton with joy for roses blown,
Who might have gleaned but weeds and rue
  Had they but known.

So little comes upon the sight
  When pent by day in golden bars,
But oh, the vistas of the night
  Beyond the stars!

DEGRADATION

Now, surely, I am twice a fool
   To break my heart by night and day
Because a woman's mocking lips
   Are turned away.

I made her throbbing songs; I said:
   "This one last time before I die
I will pour life like water out
   Nor question why."

I said: "I will burn out of me
   All lingering loves of other years
And all old bitter wisdom learned
   With bitter tears."

And now the foolishness of this:
   Though she has only scorn of me,
I think I am grown half in love
   With beggary!

LOVE IS A THIEF

Oh, break my harp when I am dead
    And burn my songs along with me
And let no foolish prayers be said
    And no long wailing, bitterly,
But, rather, when a morning star
    Blazes above the gates of God,
Remember how no roses bar
    The ways you might have trod.

And when you walk where then we met
    If, haply, you grow sad for me,
Forget that once we loved, forget
    My songs and sonnets, utterly!
And oh, for summer days and sweet
    Under the roses, while you live
Forbear the fragrance, overfleet,
    And, if you can, forgive!

TO ONE IN APRIL
WEATHER

How can I say to your heart
  What you have said to mine?
How can I paint in pale song
  Laurel and columbine
And all the flowers of April
  And the windy hills of spring —
How can I sing to your heart
  As you have learned to sing?

I'll go finger my lute, now,
  And make you gongs of fire
Rich with rhythms of old time
  And a burden of long desire.
But you that follow the lark's throat
  And pluck the eglantine —
How can I speak to your heart
  As you speak, love, to mine?

I SAID I WOULD NOT BIND ME

I said I would not bind me to be a slave of toil,
To barter youth and gladness for any golden spoil;
I said the stars were naked and the wild winds were free
And I would have a free heart to round the world with
      me.

I said I would not bind me, but one came tripping by
And there was laughter on her lip and promise in her
      eye,
And when she left the wide road I followed down a lane
To dwell among the toilers and toil among the grain.

I said I would not bind me, but I have pawned my heart
To buy a bit of farm-land, a cottage, and a cart.
And how can I forgive them, the Liar and the Lie,
That lured me from my wandering and brought me
      here to die?

SONG TO BE SAID
AT DAYBREAK

I cannot think of other things for thinking of desire
To burn a woman's brows and breast with kisses flown
      with fire;
Nor all the books of all the East and western sages' too,
Shall aught avail to comfort me while this is yet to do.

Beneath the lighted groins of night I sit and cannot
      speak
Of gargoyles wrought in Gothic stone or griffins carved
      in Greek,
But only of a woman's grace: among the stars I see
The bright and bitter beauty of a face that mocks at me.

Oh, I will be a falconer, a trainer just and wise,
And I will break my heart to hawk at bees and butter-
      flies;
And let it fly at random check or clip on lawful wings,
I'll ride the world in hunting green and think of other
      things!

TO LEAVE IN MAY

Goodby, and if you will, forget,
   There are so many men
Another's arm will comfort you
   When spring comes round again.

And you will walk beneath the trees,
   Wondering then, as now,
Why he that once has kissed your lips
   Will only kiss your brow.

The worst of women is the thing
   Which fools have found the best —
You will be true and helpless, you
   Will lie along his breast.

For you can never understand
   And he can never say,
In April it is time to love,
   But time to leave in May.

EXILE

I'll not return to Arcady
   Though you are going there,
Nay, though you beckon me to come
   With vine leaves in your hair.
The way is strange, the road is long,
   The wild west wind is cold
And I should miss a face I knew
   In Arcady of old.

I'll not return to Arcady.
   Today I saw a boy
Blow kisses to a little maid
   Who laughed in wanton joy,
And as he swaggered down the street,
   A song upon his tongue,
The whole wide world was Arcady
   To him, for he was young.

IF I REMEMBER

I think I shall not overmuch
    Be grieved, when I am old and gray,
For loss of kisses and the touch
    Of fingers on my face today;
I think I shall not care at all
    For lips or looks or any love
If only I can still recall
    The emptiness thereof.

The mouth of maiden or the mouth
    Of courtezan or wanton dame
Is always cruel as the South
    And always bitter as a flame.
I think that if I but recall
    How lips will tire that once have met
I shall not ever care at all ...
    But what if I forget?

PIQUE

Get to your priest and altar
   And get to your bridal bed
And let your lover be happy,
   What of your maidenhead!

And you shall bear him daughters
   And you shall bear him sons
And God may give you a glory
   Greater than Solomon's.

And you may never remember
   Or, haply, never forget
The dewy hands of Orion
   Belting a violet.

But I shall sleep in a palace
   Or beg my wine and bread,
For I can fiddle without you,
   You and your maidenhead!

RECONCILIATION

When I am dead and deep in dust
   So you but plant a rose-tree there
Get back to labor and to lust
   And weep no more nor greatly care.

The quick they have so much to learn,
   The dead they have so much to do,
If but your roses bloom and burn
   There shall be peace between us two.

PART TWO

We have forgotten beauty and all our Gods are good
And little we remember now the dryads and the wood,
And only old philosophers and foolish dreamers know
What lady lived in Lesbos a weary time ago.

MOUNTEBANK

When I have put my motley off
    And walk the streets like other men,
I wonder will the people scoff
    At what I have been, then.

I wonder will the people say:
    "There goes one that played the clown
With making bitter songs and gay
    All around the town."

Ah Dagonet, strike hands with me
    And tell what no man living tells —
How one puts off the infamy
    Of cap and bells.

YET AGAIN AND
YET AGAIN

Yet again and yet again there'll be those to say:
"April's in the south wind, kiss and come away!
April's in the south wind and where are we to go?
Kiss and come to church now and have your lines to
     show."

Yet again and yet again there'll be things to buy,
Satin shoes and broadcloth and beads to please the eye,
Satin shoes and broadcloth and sheets for lying-in.
Everything's to get now, and where shall one begin?

Yet again and yet again there'll be tears to shed.
All the boys are gone away, all the girls are wed.
All the boys are gone away and up and down the stairs
No one ever laughs now — seems that no one dares.

Yet again and yet again there'll be work to do.
There's the grain to harvest — and what of me and you?
There's the grain to harvest, and we'll be growing old.
Save a bit of silver now and save a bit of gold.

(cont'd., new stanza)

Yet again and yet again there'll be graves to keep,
Little graves and long graves, but all of them are deep —
Little graves and long graves — and there'll be those to
    say:
"April's in the wind now, kiss and come away!"

ROMANCE

There was a queen in Nineveh
    And there were queens in Tyre,
And Egypt had a fair queen
    As ever men desire.

Upon her throne in Camelot
    Sat burning Guinevere,
And Eleanor in Aquitaine
    With an opal on her ear.

These women are but drifting dust,
    And who is there to say
That all their loveliness and lust
    Bother men today?

But I must make a little song
    And make it fair and sweet
Because a wanton smiled at me
    A-walking down the street.

WAY OF A MAID
WITH A MAN

Daughter of Eve, daughter of Eve,
Why do you linger and languish and grieve?
Beauty is yours, even beauty to weave
  Chains for the Son of the Morning.

"Nay, there is someone who follows me not
Gone far away from this wearisome spot,
Someone who saw me and turned and forgot,
  Wherefore I weep in the morning."

Daughter of Eve, daughter of Eve,
Lo, he returns to you, he that would leave,
See how he comes with his heart on his sleeve,
  Cleaving the mists of the morning.

"Nay, I had dreamed 'twas his pleasure and plot
To force me to follow him — why did he not? —
With Eden behind us and Eden forgot,
  Into the gold of the morning."

FOR LOVE IS OF
THE VALLEY

I wonder who the woman was
    That loved him there in Galilee
Or ever he put off the garb
    Of carpentry.

And went she up to Golgotha?
    She had but little ease, I ween,
For leave to kiss his hands and feet
    With Magdalene.

Oh, better feed the flame of love
    In any sober shepherd lad
Than wither at the blazing lips
    Of one called mad.

A CHRISTMAS IDYLL

There were three mages of the East
Went bearing gifts to make a feast
  And came to Bethlehem.
The first mage brought of frankincense
Full goodly store for reverence
  In woven anadem;
The second, in his mantle's fold,
Bare beaten silver and red gold;
  Whiles for an harbinger
There flamed a strange white Star in Heaven,
Waxen more bright than planets seven;
  The third mage carrieth myrrh.

All weary in a tavern shed
Lay Mary that was brought to bed
  Of Godis only Son.
And Mary had for handmaidens
Three women that were never men's
  To wive as all men wonn.

(cont'd., no new stanza)

45

Two damsels were right fair and sweet,
The third wore over hands and feet
  Amber from sea-side ta'en;
And Mary's cloke was soft with fur
And a gold girdle belted her
  Of writhen serpents twain.

Three mages stand upon the straw.
They lifted up their eyne and saw
  The Blessed Babe; and laid
Down treasures of bright Eastern kings —
Spikenard and gems and finger-rings
  And pearls and purple and jade —
Whereat a golden beam of light
Fell in slant wise athwart the night
  And Angels thronged thereon
Came caroling from the Halls of Heaven,
"Lo, unto us a Child is given
  And unto us a Son!"

AND ONE WITH
SECRET TEARS

When high at noon Apollo rides
    Before the eyes of men,
Unseen above her seething tides,
    Who speaks of Luna, then?

A man shall die and, lost to creeds,
    Forget his dreams and fears,
And one shall mourn in widow's weeds
    And one with secret tears.

RENUNCIATION

Roses are a dead delight
    When upon the wind they wave,
Since I found them, red and white,
    Where they grew upon thy grave.

Kisses are a dead desire,
    Strange as water after wine,
Since I drained the icy fire
    From those pale dead lips of thine.

MOOD

I awake and hear the rain
   On the sounding cells of night
Like a threnody of pain
   For dead delight.

Shall I wake and turn again
   To that song above my head,
Shall I ever hear the rain
   When I am dead?

I WOULD
REMEMBER
CONSTANT THINGS

The little broken bones of men
    They ride on every wind that blows,
With dust of Memphis whirled again
    And this year's dust of last year's rose;
The little bitter tears of men
    They are but drops in the salt sea,
Lost forever beyond all ken
    Of flesh like you and me.

And though from mountains worn away
    I mix the mortar for my house
And build within the light of day
    For studious ease and long carouse,
The rain shall beat above my head,
    The wind shall rattle my bolted door,
And all the ghosts of all the dead
    Shall pace my fire-lit floor.

(cont'd., new stanza)

Yet I will fashion greater Gods
    For Lares now, than other men;
I would forget how Sirius plods
    Through galaxies and back again;
I would remember constant things,
    As sleep whereof no dreams affray,
Before the wind on wandering wings
    Has blown my bones away.

A LAMENT

Over the lake my lad has gone,
    Over the lake at the dawn of day,
And the waves they follow and fall and fawn
    And the children chatter, as children may,
And I sit and think, as the sun goes down
    In the mists of Michigan's western sea.
For what of the dreams he takes to town?
    And what of the dreams he leaves with me?

Over the lake my lad has gone
    As the sun must go at the close of day,
And the waves they tumble and roll and fawn
    And the elders gossip, as elders may,
And I sit thinking, as light by light
    The windows look to the western sea —
Dear God, be good to my lad tonight!
    And oh, be merciful unto me!

THE KINGS THAT FOUGHT FOR HELEN

The kings that fought for Helen
    Are gone like ghosts away
And all their wars are done now,
    And all their lusts, for aye;
But he that harped for Helen,
    His fingers strike and strum,
Though Helen's hands are dust, now,
    And Helen's lips are dumb.

And I dream dreams of Helen,
    As men shall dream for aye
Till all the prayers are said, then,
    And all the Gods are gray,
For that the loves of Helen
    In so sweet words were sung
When Helen's grave was green then,
    And Helen's fame was young.

ONE DAY

As I went out through Michigan, went motoring out
  through Michigan
  Where deep the dark Muskegon ran to seek its west-
    ern sea,
I heard a song that filled the dawn, the radiant, ramp-
    ant, golden dawn —
  "Into the west my lad has gone, who will remember
    me?"
Oh, blue the lakes of Michigan, blue as the skies of
    Michigan,
  And blue were the eyes of Marianne who sang that
    lover's lay,
Yellow as corn her blowing hair (the sun was a glory on
    her hair)
  And ruddy her lips when, halting there, I kissed the
    song away.

I know the woods of Michigan and all the hills of
    Michigan,
  And never shall I forget that Pan still pipes a pagan
    lay,

(cont'd., no new stanza)

And never shall I forget the wind (the grass of the
      upland knows the wind),
  Luring the lazy clouds of Ind over the world away.
But red were the lakes of Michigan, red as the skies
      of Michigan,
  And red were the eyes of Marianne who wept where
      none could see
When I drove into the sunset glow, the windy, welter-
      ing, western glow,
  And oh, the burden of pride, and oh, the ache of a
      dream in me!

SONG FOR THE SAKE OF SINGING

There'll be April down the wind and I'll be gone away,
I'll be out of the light of time until the Judgment Day,
And May will come and June will go, as you and I
      have kenned,
But I'll be hidden away, my love, forever until the end.
And little enough shall men recall the songs that I
      have penned,
And little enough my heart will care if I have sleep
      to friend,
For I am tired of all the world and only now I pray
There'll be April down the wind when I am gone away.

Oh, there'll be April down the wind and a melody
      grave or gay
Throbbing over the drums of rain and through the
      viols of day,
For God must live and God must love and God must
      have his ease
Though all the men of the whirling worlds lie drowned
      within the seas.

(cont'd., no new stanza)

And never again shall tears be shed for the drunken
    souls of these,
And never shall death be gained away with gold at
    godly knees,
But you shall come and they shall come and all shall
    weep and say:
"There'll be April down the wind, but I'll be gone
    away!"

SONG BEFORE
DYING

Now loose the silver cord and break
    The golden bowl, the golden bowl,
Sing me a song to quiet my heart
    And let the night come down!
For life is over the winds away
    And bells may chime or bells may toll —
Where is the sound of the grinding now
    That throbbed in the streets of town?

Where is the sound of the grinding now
    When mills are old, when mills are old?
Drums are dumb in the tents of the kings
    And the silks are torn with time
And the mouths of the laughing girls are mute
    (Where are the loves their lips have told?)
And only out of the whispered years
    Murmurs an endless rhyme.

Only out of the whispered years,
    Remembered well, remembered well,

(cont'd., no new stanza)

Moves a melody ghostly gay
 To a burden of youth's desire.
Horns are wound in the mystic hills
 Where Death's abroad with the hounds of Hell —
O God, give back to the minstrel now
 One song to his ancient lyre!

RUSTIC

When I rose up at morning
   My heart was glad and gay.
I went across the farmlands
   To sell some corn and hay,
And there I met a gypsy lass
   A-loitering into town
With laughing lips and wanton hips
   And eyes of blazing brown.

When I sat down at noontime
   To eat my simple fare
Oh, then there passed a gypsy lad
   With a rose upon his hair.
He paused and fiddled a song or two,
   The children danced in glee,
Then he was down and out of the town
   Under the greenwood tree.

When I came home at sundown
   My deary at the door
She bade me gentle welcome
   And placed a meal before.

(cont'd., no new stanza)

But what care I for home now
    And what care I for ease?
My heart's away across the day
    And out beyond the seas!

SAILOR SONG

Let others break sod when the robins are nesting
  And sow for the harvest in valley and plain,
My heart of a rover is wild to be breasting
  The surge of the surf and the might of the main.
When the tang of the spring, like the sting of white
        spray,
Comes to lure me and call me and dare me away,
Oh, it's ho! for the ropes and the sails they'll be test-
        ing —
  I'm off to the sea in the wind and the rain!

Let others sing songs of the joys of the byways,
  The trysts in the gloaming, the lays of the lark,
Let others delight in the throngs on the highways,
  The bustle and babble from dawn unto dark.
The droning of bees and the murmur of crowds
Are drowned in the hymn of the hum of the shrouds
And it's ho! for a ship to go booming down my ways,
  A sloop or a schooner, a brig or a bark.

(cont'd., new stanza)

Let others for wealth or for wisdom be sighing,
　　The world it is wide and the ways they are free,
And today is today but tomorrow means dying,
　　And what shall the money-bags matter to me?
Oh, it's ho and it's hey and it's hey and it's ho!
There are women and wine in the tavern, I know,
But it's ho! for the skies where the gray gulls are fly-
　　　　ing —
　　I'm over the hills to the ships and the sea!

CITY BRED

Now count me out in silver
   The wages I have won,
And I'll go buy a good cigar,
   A glass of beer and a bun,
And I'll go down the harbor
   To watch the riding lights
Of ships that lie at anchor there
   While men lie warm o' nights.

And there's the Molly Brander
   That's in from River Plate,
Her skipper was the carpenter,
   Her bosun acting mate;
And there's the Empress Olga
   Come home from lands of gold
With ivory and parakeets
   And ebony in her hold.

(cont'd., new stanza)

64

The riding lights at anchor
    They tell their tales of life
That never men shall understand
    Who keep with child and wife,
The riding lights at anchor
    They tell their tales of death
That sailors only talk about
    Drunk and with bated breath.

So count me out in silver
    The wages I have won,
And I'll be off along the wharves
    To see how tides may run.
For though I come at morning
    And toil the livelong day,
By night I go a-sailing O
    Around the world away!

WHALER'S CHANTEY

We've said goodby to our dearies,
  We've laid tobaccy in store,
We're startin' a three-year whalin' cruise
  From Hell to Singapore;
The wind is over the quarter,
  The banks are under our lee —
Heave — O! Tail onto a sheet,
  We're standin' out to sea!

Her fo'c's'le's painted with whitewash,
  Her hold is pumped out dry,
There's empty barrels atween decks
  An' the boats are nested high;
There's mebbe a thousan' fish to catch
  An' a lump of ambergree —
An' the ol' tub carries a bone in her teeth
  A-snorin' down to sea!

There's gals a-plenty in Boston
  Will moor you if they can,

(cont'd., no new stanza)

66

But seldom a gal can ride it out
    With a rovin' sailor-man.
Oh, the wind is over the quarter,
    The banks are under our lee —
Heave — O! Tail onto a sheet,
    We're standin' out to sea!

A WANDER SONG

Emerald seas and seas of agate wandering under the
    sky,
And I would loiter the world around or ever I come to
    die —
Or ever I come to die, love, and to say farewell to you —
With only a cook and a cabin boy and a lazy Lascar
    crew.

They've amber sands in the coral isles and little or no
    restraint,
And God has painted the misty hills as only God can
    paint,
As only God can paint, love, where the copra schooners
    ply
Through emerald seas and seas of agate wandering
    under the sky.

A bulbul sobs in a citron tree that blooms in Samarcand
And the song of a Sufi haunts the night for those who
    understand,

(cont'd., no new stanza)

For those who understand, love, and the hidden lutes
    reply,
And I would loiter the world around or ever I come
    to die.

Oh, I would barter my goods away and I would leave
    mine ease
To follow the gull and the albatross in the winds that
    walk the seas,
In the winds that walk the seas, love, with a lazy Lascar
    crew,
Or ever I come to die, love, and to say farewell to you.

OLD SHIPS

The merchandise of all the earth
   Was theirs to bear: the merchandise
Of autumn-scented wine for mirth
   In man's eyes and in woman's eyes
And all wrought ivory, white like milk
   And gold and silver and soft silk
And curious amber flecked with mist
   And oil and wool and amethyst.

The ships of Carthage and the ships
   Of Tyre about the windy seas
From isles of Ind where honey drips
   To the far Cimbric Chersonese,
And Rome's triremes of saffron sails,
   With girls to grace an emperor's feast,
And Spanish galleons big with bales,
   And junks of all the lecherous East. . . .

Their bones are bleached on shimmering coasts,
   At broken wharves they reek and rot,
They walk the seas like grimly ghosts
   Of dead men out of days forgot.

(cont'd., no new stanza)

Old ships, old ships! The merchandise
    Of all the earth was theirs to bear
When they were flown with enterprise
    And their dark hulls were fair.

MELODY

Shall I be tellin' ye secrets?
    Shall I be tellin' ye lies?
It's divil a bit I care now
    For Kate Maloney's eyes.
For Kate's a mother of childer
    An' I've been over the sea,
But och, the trouble an' loneliness
    When last she looked at me!
I mind the wind was a whisper,
    The moon was kissin' the hill,
An' all the people of Ireland
    Were sleepin' soft an' still;
For I was a broth of a boy, then,
    An' I mind her eyes were wet;
And divil a bit I care for Kate,
    But I wisht I could forget!

WILD

When I was young and handsome
   A lady loved me well,
And whether it was wise to go,
   Who is there to tell?
But soon I rose and left her
   And looked in other eyes,
For liberty is more than faith
   And beauty more than lies.

When I was young and handsome
   (And that was long ago),
I might have been a richer man,
   One lady loved me so;
But I have marched with legions
   And sailed the seas in ships;
For life is more than husbandry
   And love than woman's lips.

OF MIST AND AIR

The Gods are old and sad and wise,
    Since they were made by aged men
For whom desire in woman's eyes
    And madness would not come again.
The Gods are cold and grave and stern,
    Wrought marvelously of mist and air —
Though roses bloom and roses burn
    Sweet as a woman's hair!

Young lips will fasten hard on lips,
    Young hearts will brave through turbulent seas;
Song and the ways of tall swift ships
    And wild swift words are dear to these.
Vanity, vanity! All things pass,
    Lost in the wars of wind and wave —
And who hath seen beneath the grass
    A God's hand reached to save?

Oh, choice of follies! Give me now
    To swagger through romantic streets
As he that paints Aspasia's brow
    On every laughing wench he meets!

(cont'd., no new stanza)

Give me my bubbling veins again,
   May's madness and May's mystery,
And all the Gods of all old men
   May part and cease to be!

BLIND

The throbbing of the city is like lions,
Like lions roaring at sunset in old Rome,
Being hungry in their dungeons or being sad
For their unbounded midnights; Ah, the color,
The splendor and the color of the city!

There must be beauty thronged in costly silks,
Delicious beauty of women come to buy
Sables and sapphires, and there must be men
Going in swift cars proudly and having gold
To scatter and wearing purple and green and gold.

And surely there are gardens beyond walls
Where there are many roses and where girls
With garlanded hair and laughter and wine-wet lips
Dance before little temples and where lovers
Walk in dark avenues carpeted with stars.

A surf gnars on the beaches. Are there not ships
Big bellied and strange come over the world's rim?
Ah, wandering ships with peacocks and black slaves
And ships borne down by copper and silver ingots?
Are there not princess' barges there and queens'?

(cont'd., new stanza)

Bells ring out in the city, bells that call
Like trumpets, and there must be warriors there.
For surely there are battles in the earth
And beautiful men gone fighting with bright swords,
And somewhere in the sunlight kings are dying!

A LADY LIVED IN LESBOS

A lady lived in Lesbos a weary time ago;
So many years have overpassed it's little we can know;
So many wars have worn away, with Gods and creeds
      and kings,
It's little we remember now of older, happier things.

For men go up and down the land, under and over the
      seas
(A lady lived in Lesbos, but what is that to these?)
And men sit watching, night by night, how Mars the
      planet spins
And women sit and gossip over marriages and sins.

We have forgotten beauty and all our Gods are good
And little we remember now the dryads and the wood,
And only old philosophers and foolish dreamers know
What lady lived in Lesbos a weary time ago.

THE STREETS OF HELL

When I go down the streets of Hell,
Go swaggering down the streets of Hell,
   Then I shall see the great ones pass
     In gorgeous golden cars —
Bonaparte and Prester John
And Charlemagne and Genghis Khan
   And all the glorious kings — alas! —
     That passed beneath the stars.

And only on the streets of Hell,
The murky, turbulent streets of Hell,
   Shall I behold the blood-red curls
     Of slain Semiramis,
Pompadour and the priceless tear
That Arthur loved as Guinevere
   And all the wonderful wanton girls
     That damned a king with a kiss.

IN PASSING

There was a road a-winding, a little road a-winding,
    And over hills and under hills it led me far away
Past barley fields and hamlets and busy mills a-grinding,
    And came upon a city at the closing of the day —
    The burnished roofs were blinding at the closing of
       the day.

There was a woman weaving, a silent woman weaving,
    She sat within a shop door and she raised her eyes
       to mine;
And suddenly the clamor was hushed beyond believing
    And all the air was pleasant for the smell of eglantine.
    And all her face was grieving for the smell of eglan-
       tine.

It was the time when roses, when fettered, redolent roses
    Are shaken by the freedom of some passionate night-
       ingale
That wantons from a hillside and through a garden's
       closes,
    Singing of Mytilene or a lovely Theban vale —
    Where Itylus reposes in a lovely Theban vale.

(cont'd., new stanza)

We two are long in sunder, forever now in sunder,
    For many roads of many lands have led me far away,
But always I shall fancy, or over hills or under,
    I see a silent woman at the closing of the day.
    What does she weave, I wonder, at the closing of the
        day?

IN BABYLON, IN BABYLON

In Babylon, in Babylon
   They made a harlot queen,
And all the gold of all the world
   Was gathered there, I ween,
And love was always young, there,
   And beauty always gay
Upon the streets of Babylon,
   Before they passed away.

In Babylon, in Babylon
   It was a queen's delight
To seek along the dark ways
   For lovers in the night;
And men they came in armor
   And men they came in skins
To eat the meats of Babylon
   And sip the wine of sins.

(cont'd., new stanza)

In Babylon, in Babylon
    The walls are fallen down
And gone are all the princes
    And merchants of the town,
The little laughing ladies
    And lords of bitter wars
In all the halls of Babylon
    Are quiet as the stars.

THEN COMETH
ATROPOS

When first I went to London
   My heart and hopes were high
And there was not in all the town
   A man so proud as I,
And Beauty smiled upon me
   And Wealth did not ignore,
When first I went to London
   And called at Fortune's door.

When next I went to London
   I rode as kings may ride,
So there was not in all the land
   A greater man beside,
And Beauty bowed before me
   And Wealth could but implore,
When next I went to London
   And mused at Fortune's door.

When last I went to London
   With darkness on mine eyes,

(cont'd., no new stanza)

84

Oh, there was not in all the world
   A man more deeply wise,
Yet Beauty laughed and left me
   And Wealth stalked on before,
When last I went to London
   And fawned at Fortune's door.

A DRINKING SONG

Gather ye, gather ye round!
    Let winter blow over the chimney!
Gather ye, gather ye round!
    Fill tankards and mugs to the brim, nay,
Here's health to the feeble and strength to the strong,
And life it is short and the grave it is long,
So drink while you can, sir, and sing me a song!
    Come round, round, round!

Gather ye, gather ye round!
    Here's cheer for your trouble and sorrow!
Gather ye, gather ye round!
    The devil may care for tomorrow!
All ye that must labor for knight or for knave,
There's little to gain and there's little to save,
And never a song nor a drink in the grave!
    Come round, round, round!

I'LL RUN NO MORE

The moon is only a moon now,
    And the mist is only mist;
The lips of the roses on my brow
    But kiss as they always kissed;
And arms of women of high degree,
    Though heavy with gifts of gold,
Not always fetter the dreams of me,
    For I am growing old.

I'll run no more in the fierce dawn
    And I'll strike my harp no more,
The foolish lovers across the lawn
    But stroll as they strolled of yore,
The tales of battle and might of men
    And the wonderful songs were sung
Shall never be quite the same again —
    Oh, God! — for I was young!

DESERTED

The moon above the snows tonight
　　Is soft and sad for nights of spring,
But in my window burns a light
　　And one there is that's wandering.

And shall I wait or shall I go?
　　For here there is no helpful thing;
But there's a path across the snow
　　And one there is that's wandering.

And oh, it's lonesome in the ground
　　With none to laugh and none to sing
Nor any scent nor any sound!
　　And one there is that's wandering.

PROPHECY

There shall be kings again to ride
   The chariots of countless wars
And build of porphyry and jade
   Vast palaces beneath the stars.

There shall be nobles proud and grim
   In insolence of blazonries
And women beautiful for sin
   And wines of many vintages.

And time shall dance his rigadoon
   On ivory and amber dials.
And there shall be great singers, then,
   And music torn from virgin viols.

PART THREE

For sometime I was King of these Black Isles,
Crowned gloriously with honor and with love.

THE KING OF THE BLACK ISLES

Pale in the silver armor of its dreams
The soul loves not to wake within the night
Where, haply, but one watchful candle gleams
Between what threatening shadows dare the light,
But, rather, strives with all it may of might
To hold the magic battlements of sleep
Which look upon wide valleys, rich and bright
And happy homes and herds and rivers deep
And fountains of desire from which men wake and weep.

To wake and weep — that, surely, is a thing
Which all men suffer under the old stars,
Since all men born are born to sorrowing
In quiet days, remembering splendid wars,
Though woman's eyes become swift avatars
Flamed marvelously across mysterious ways
And summer sighs among the deodars
With perfume of a passion that betrays,
Low on a secret bed, her rose-rapt nights and days.

(cont'd., new stanza)

Bound in the silken scents of night, I slept
Upon a cloud of melody that rose
From aloes and from almond trees and swept
Over the couch, not breaking my repose,
But flinging on my dream such mist as flows
From censers hung along the walls of Heaven
And drugs us out of time and space and blows
Infinity within our ken and even
That ecstasy of peace to which the Gods are given.

Was it some bulbul fainter than the rest,
Luring my heart to follow his wild throat,
That stilled the burdened pulses in my breast
With loss of louder music, note by note?
Was it that streaming loveliness remote,
Like opals poured from pitchers of deep glass,
Which, ending in a sudden silence, smote
Hard on my ear as clangor of fierce brass?
Ah, harder in the dark for beauty that must pass!

Ah, no! It was the sound of whispering
Where slaves within the chamber chanted shame,
Whimpering out of dread that I, the King,
Might wake before a woman turned and came
Unto her bed and mine . . . ah, she whose name
My young pride blazoned over ancient walls
What time I brought her — feather of my fame! —
To share my throne and fill my fathers' halls
With laughter clear as dryads' at sylvan waterfalls.

(cont'd., new stanza)

For sometime I was King of these Black Isles,
Crowned gloriously with honor and with love.
My realm was bounded by unmeasured miles,
My gold was as the unnumbered sands thereof;
Before my throne all men bowed down, above
Reigned the sweet voice of my soul's ortolan
So trusted as one trusts a nesting dove . . .
How could I dream she played the courtezan?
Yet see me what I am — half marble and half man!

They wantoned in the garden. On his breast
Her bosom, all white lilies on black fur,
Moved and her mouth moved, sobbing without rest
For thirst of love that would not ease in her.
She drank down kisses as the wine-bibber
Drinks from long cups and ever cries out "More!"
Till I, who stood with trembling scimiter,
Marveled and mused and for a time forebore
To deal them death, for shame of being their auditor.

I know not whence it is, but in wild love
There is a kind of grandeur, as if then
The soul flings off all flesh and fear thereof,
Striding out naked in the sight of men.
Who pause and stand a little in awe, as when
They look on courage moving with calm breath
And high, stern heart upon some denizen
Of darkness and the doubtful caves of death,
Serene of faith in honor and in honor's faith.

(cont'd., new stanza)

What angel or what evil unknown djinn,
Ranging from midmost regions of the air,
Found out her woman's heart to wander in
And ruin us with reign of madness there?
Could not her eyes foresee their own despair?
Was she not privy to what dangers lay
But in a whisper, in a slave's wan stare,
When all the palace marked her face betray
A night's fierce fires of love yet smoldering through
    the day?

Ah, God, she was delightful unto me!
Her breasts were fashioned for kissing all night long;
Smoother than amber burnished by the sea
The arches of her feet were smooth and strong;
Her hair was woven of silken flame and song;
Her mouth more bruised for honey than honeycomb;
And on her brows lay no more shadow of wrong
Than on the sails of laden ships blown home,
Far out of spice-rapt lands, on waves flung white with
    foam.

Exquisite in my garden of dead kings
Her beauty burned along some fountain's brim
Like fire of gems in heavy golden rings,
Like rubies in a God's eyes, hallowing him;
Her curious garments whispered, limb to limb,
How all that body bore them in proud grace
Or in the glade of tamarinds, deep and dim,
Or loitering on the dusty market-place —
Even through a woman's veils, men marked the royal
    race.

(cont'd., new stanza)

I made a wondrous palace on this wise:
The floors wrought well of onyx and sweet wood,
The walls of jasper, and I bade devise
High, delicate roofs that pictured all things good;
One room was saffron and one red like blood
And every room was entered through glad gold;
And pleasant for light breezes, though day stood
Blazing his wrath against the nether cold,
The courts about those halls murmured how long waves
    rolled.

Damascus sent us diamonds; from the North
Came caravans with sapphires; caravans
Across the sands of Syria issued forth
With silks and silver and spikenard; in sedans
Litters of leopards; jade and amber fans;
Soft skins of lambs and brilliant skins of birds;
And, silent, but with sunnier soul than man's,
Came apes from watching tropic moons like curds
Churned in the vats of time by Gods too wise for words.

Beauty being dead, what shall be said of her
More than men say of dead men who were just?
"One hour he had for music and for myrrh
Or ever within the worm-worn grave was thrust,
One hour for labor and a little lust
Before time quenched his passion in decay."
And who would seek to stir the unheeding dust?
And who would have one further word to say?
Ere he make end of saying, he shall be borne away.

(cont'd., new stanza)

Now, therefore, it may well be said that bliss
And all high beauty are no more to us
Than deep remembrance of a dead rose is
Which, in dead days, a live thing tremulous,
Burned in the hair of one made glorious
With kisses sown thick over brows and breast,
For as all passion passes, even thus
Romance, with velvet fingers of unrest,
Paints in the chrome of tears our lost loves loveliest.

It is as if one riding to the night
Looks back at some tall city and forgets
The fetid ways, the squalor and the sight
Of base men bowed to brutal epithets
In watching those far towers and minarets
Springing to golden domes magnificent
With banners billowing on wide parapets,
While rings from battlement and battlement
The clang of trumpets blown for some young king's
    ascent.

Oh, then, farewell forever all desire!
Farewell delight! And radiant reign farewell!
I see the red west embered on the pyre
Of day's long glory, slain by Azrael
Who walks in plumes, a dusky sentinel,
Down all the lingering vistas of the light
With emblems of his empery — asphodel
And silver — and there closes on my sight
The gloom of wings and all the mystery of night.

BEFORE DAWN

Guinevere to Lancelot:

This is the last time we shall ever meet.
This is the last time, lying against thy feet,
   With hair let down like gold strewn over them,
My fingers and my lips will touch thee, sweet.

Ah, hold me close and closer! Comfort me
With kisses pressed across the long lone sea
   That even now sweeps, tide on surging tide,
Between me and my longing after thee!

How swift the moon runs down the sky tonight!
Like a white doe hunted by dogs of light.
   And all the color and wonder of the world
Will pass with these last hours of her flight.

And when the sonnets of the nightingales
Have ended in the thickets in the swales
   The dawn will course above an empty earth
And all our loves will be as old wives' tales.

(cont'd., new stanza)

For never, though I live a thousand years,
Shall prayer avail nor magic of deep tears
　　To break my heart for kisses down my breast
Or for thy fancied footsteps in my ears.

And never, should we meet again in hall
By chance of travel or as war may fall,
　　Can we spring soul to soul, as in the time
Moment by moment going beyond recall.

Dost thou remember how, upon a day
When all the land burned blithely into May,
　　A clump of spears came glancing to my gate
And thou made'st one — and there was naught to say?

For, seeing thee afar off, in my heart
I had said truly where I leaned, apart:
　　"God help me now if thou art not the King!
And oh, God help me if indeed thou art!"

Oh, gold upon a warrior's helm by day,
Oh, steel borne swiftly down the King's highway,
　　Oh, banners blown along the woods like flame,
Oh, youth gone riding in the month of May!

The hazel and the hawthorne and the pine,
The violet's purple and the purple vine —
　　Dost thou remember, O my friend? And oh,
The windy hillsides fired with eglantine?

(cont'd., new stanza)

And thus by mountain mere and woodland grot
And many a Druid shrine to Gods forgot,
    Till, flung along the sunset, royally,
Golden with glory, the towers of Camelot.

Ah, then, the days at banquet where the King
Pledged all his knights, the roofs re-echoing,
    And thy grave eyes poured kisses in my cup
For our own revels, wing to secret wing!

Ah, then, the elfin music of the horns
Wound in the woods away on hunting morns
    When hearts went pagan, hearing on the wind
Daughters of Odin singing of the Norns!

And ah, the violent splendor of the lists
And Dagonet dancing, hawks on motley wrists,
    While thou and Tristram, Gawain and Geraint
Fought for my snood of pearls and amethysts!

I would our lives were over! Oh, would God
We two were lying under the cold sod
    With rain and sun and snow thrown over us
Forever as the seasons may be shod!

Would God the winds had blown us out of time
And all regret of roses and of rime
    And winnowed us among the mocking stars
Farther than ever dreams have dared to climb!

(cont'd., new stanza)

Would God, would God the seas of all the years
Broke over us with salter waves than tears!
   That all the earth of mountains weighed us down
Deeper in silence than the rolling spheres!

But this is madness! Must I harrow thee
With idle lamentation, seeing that we
   Have kissed our souls together? O my love,
Lie still a little longer! Bear with me!

Once, long ago, when thou wast with the King
Far in some pagan realm adventuring,
   I lay within my chamber, wanting sleep —
Indeed, I cannot well resolve this thing!

Methought there came an Ancient through the wall,
The stones and arras parting not at all,
   Bearing a wrinkled parchment and a staff,
An older man than any in Arthur's hall.

How long time passed I know not. Head to head
We stared. I could not know if he were dead,
   Till, speaking in a great low voice of doom,
"Mordred!" the windy echoes murmured " — dred!"

It was a night in winter. No man stirred,
No scent of flower nor any song of bird,
   And only the fierce wolf-hound on the hearth
Growled in his sleep as he had something heard.

(cont'd., new stanza)

Ah, Mordred, son of Morgawse! Wilt thou yet
Have tears and death and ruin for a debt
Paid over with deep penance long ago
Or ever the King was crowned or me had met?

Must I, whose face lured Arthur from desire
Of his own sister's body, purge in fire
   And heartbreak all the secret shames and sins
Thy mother made at incest, and thy sire?

It might have been forever but for thee,
And Lancelot still the prince of chivalry,
   Wearing my favor through a courtly world
With none to leer, devising infamy.

It might have been that God had pitied us
Some day when days are ended, meaning thus
   To leave our souls together, though in Hell
With lords and other ladies glorious.

Ah, there with lovely vestals that were hurled
From rock Tarpeian in the Roman world,
   Amestris, Hero, and the great fair Queen
Semiramis, with king-kissed hair uncurled.

There Phryne and the knight Hyperides.
God knoweth they get no good days, now, nor ease,
   But how oh, better than dividing streets
Thronged wide through golden Heaven is Hell to these!

      (cont'd., new stanza)

I think that Holy Mary must forgive
All lovers who are parted and yet live,
   That our dear Lord some penance will remit
To those amerced in love renunciative.

For now our dream is over and our days
Brought to the weary round of one who lays
   Unceasing prayers before the feet of Christ,
Yet doubts the worth of that for which he prays.

For, having parted, never, though we meet
Hereafter, can we any more entreat
   The old unbroken innocence of love
When no man else was brave nor woman sweet.

There should be always something like a wraith
Lurking along the shadowy halls of faith
   Till passion fled and left us stammering there
With dreams gone strange and evil unto death.

Grown weary of long war and sick at heart
Man may forget a woman when, apart,
   She throweth no more a glamor over him
And nearer beauty burneth with newer art;

Since he that loveth woman loveth much
The bending of her body and the touch
   And all the delicate perfume of her hair
And tenderness — he loveth even such.

(cont'd., new stanza)

And hast thou loved me better? Whether it is
My lips have gleaned a glory from thy kiss
    Or whether thy great soul was matched with mine
When God made all things first — I know not this.

But think'st thou that, another's concubine,
I would break bread with Arthur or drain wine?
    But that thou'rt more than God's fair face to me,
I would play traitor to thy King and mine?

When thou goest from me, having said farewell,
Thou leavest me awhile in utter Hell!
    How shall I love again, O Lancelot,
Who shall have sometime lain on asphodel?

And if tonight there is no ghost, I ween,
Nor any God or Devil to contravene
    The kisses of thy mouth across my throat,
Nor any flesh of man to come between,

Must hungry lips that only thine allay
Cling to the empty breasts of yesterday,
    As poor thin babes' in famine-stricken lands,
To mothers fallen down dead beside the way?

Is there no comfort more in gathering years
Than hearts resigned and sodden ash of fears,
    Where once the wild fires ravaged all the soul
In ever-lengthening intervals of tears?

(cont'd., new stanza)

Must I from April's coronals come to wear
Dark rue for secret windings in my hair
   And still forego thy splendor and thy fame?
My punishment is more than I can bear!

No more to sit among my maids and dream
Where roses brush the breast of some still stream
   Like rubies hung upon a girl's white throat,
Forming thy blazonry in every gleam.

No more to pluck from harpstrings tears of song
Not made by bards for all the wan wild throng,
   But sweetly bitter couplets to an air
Rung far from bells of silence all night long.

No more, ah, nevermore! to watch for thee
Riding from distant wars victoriously.
The color of all my life is drab with death!
My glory is departed! Comfort me!

Lancelot to Guinevere:

Lady and love, as sails of some far ship,
Blown to the west at sunset, rise and dip,
   Crimson and golden over golden seas,
Thy wild words burn and vanish at thy lip.

Since thou wilt have it so, this is the end.
That we shall meet no more, O, God forfend!
   But love and all fair ways and words of love —
With these we shall have naught to make or mend.

(cont'd., new stanza)

Nay, O thou beauty of the world! what more
Have we to tell each other? What old score
    Of kisses forfeit unto angers past?
Or what last vows wrung from us at the door?

Or ever his father gets him, man is dead.
He speaks not neither hears what things are said.
    Singing with swords go battles up and down,
But nothing recks he, then, of armies' tread.

And when the lancehead of some younger knight,
Thrust over shield, hath ended sound and sight,
    Let war blaze ever through the king-starred earth,
He shall not rise nor smitten be nor smite.

The summer will come back with all the hills
Rolling in green to meads of daffodils,
    And idle flocks gone grazing in the sun
And bird songs bickering over sylvan rills.

The grape will burn to glory and the oak
Revel in opals flaming down his cloak
    While, gold within the autumn, gold with grain,
The fields will rest in thin blue veils of smoke.

Again high halls will roar with song, again
There will be lights and feasting among men,
    Though winter ride the wind on wings of ice
And wolves howl nearer from their foodless fen.

(cont'd., new stanza)

But, silent in the sepulchre, no more
Shall man rise up from sleeping on the floor
    Nor look upon the earth's face flushed with spring
Nor lift the long bars lightly from his door.

Yet not with us hereafter as hath been
With those whom beauty hath not entered in.
    Somehow my dust will drift where thine is laid,
Somewhere my soul rejoin thee and re-win!

We have been beautiful. Till time is done
And all men cease from singing 'neath the sun,
    There shall be songs in hovel and in hall
Rhyming our meetings over, one by one.

Not glory nor the mighty fames of kings
Beat through the storms of time on tireless wings
    As love's tales flown down centuries and far
Out of dim days and proud, mysterious things.

Death and the stars keep silence! But the wind
Whispers forever of some isle or Ind
    Where once the years flung fever in their cup
Whose names are magic, having sighed and sinned.

Wherefore I think that, childless as thou art,
Thou shalt have yet some comfort when we part,
    Seeing that men will link us, name to name,
Down all the deathless histories of the heart.

(cont'd., new stanza)

It shall not be with us as it must be
With lovers lost beyond some unknown sea
   And no man saith the glory of their days.
We shall not pass to silence. Comfort thee!

BEAUTY

O Beauty, thou Goddess Immortal,
    There is none other like to thee, none!
We grave many names on thy portal,
    But the gold is not fallen from one.
Thou art served and the flame of thine altars
    Fed full by the king and the clod
And a priest of thy word never palters,
    Unknowable God!

Thou goest in robes of the morning
    A Light and a Mystery, thou.
The galaxy gleams for adorning
    The locks of thine infinite brow.
Man lives not who does not adore thee
    Whether Jupiter, Jesus or Thor
Be the image he bows to before thee,
    Serene Avatar!

Thou hast cloven the mountains in sunder
    And crowned them with chrysolite crowns;
Thou ringest the bells of the thunder;
    The seas are flung white at thy frowns;

(cont'd., no new stanza)

Thou hast not to do with our seeming
  From the womb to the wave or the sod,
But alone of thy grace is our dreaming,
  Invisible God!

For love of thee men are begotten
  Who brand their begetting as sin,
But these thou hast lost and forgotten,
  To thy porches they shall not go in;
They shall wander in chaos forever,
  They shall bitterly pray for thy ruth,
O just and inflexible Giver
  Of glimpses of truth!

Thy votaries, pale as from poring
  Over mysteries wrought in thy name,
Come forth of thy temples, adoring,
  With fingers and lips dropping flame.
Beaten down by the light of thy station,
  Overawed by thine axes and rods,
We rise but to pour thee libation,
  O Goddess of Gods!

From sistrum and lyre thou has shaken
  The sounds that were gendered in thee,
All the laughter of nymphs overtaken,
  All the thunder that sings in the sea.
We have caught from the fire of thy singing
  Such embers of passion as flame
Through the last constellations where, winging,
  Young Gods bear thy name.

(cont'd., new stanza)

Out of darkness thou givest to shame us
    Dim fabrics and delicate things
That were woven in centuries famous
    For glory of delicate kings,
Carved vessels of gold and all manner
    Of silver wrung virgin from fire
And velariums, banner on banner,
    In purple of Tyre.

Almost of thy might thou persuadest
    The triumph from tombs and the sting
From death, seeing thou never fadest,
    But risest, O Phoenix! in spring.
Almost thou wilt have us remember
    The old legends of earth and the dream
That after the flame and the ember
    The soul is supreme.

And we that have lain upon roses
    And drunk of the lethe of love,
What more can we ask, as life closes,
    Of Fates underneath or above?
What more than soft arms and bright bosoms
    Whereon to grow sated and sleep
With a wreath on the brows of such blossoms
    As Naiads may reap?

(cont'd., new stanza)

For most thou hast made of thine image
    In waters that ceaselessly roll
From ages forgot to that dim age
    When man shall at last be a soul,
Oh, most thou hast left us reflected,
    Of all we can picture of thee,
In a brothel, a hell unsuspected —
    The depths of the sea.

Yea, scented with summer and spices
    That never have trembled with cold,
Thou, Beauty, hast wrought thy devices
    On islands and inlands of gold
Where, deep over decks that were gory
    For woman or gem or doubloon,
The waves to the winds tell a story,
    The winds to the moon.

What ghosts of great ships from far places,
    Weighed down with rich burdens of bales!
What dreams and ambitions! What faces
    Of virgins denuded of veils!
What captives more lovely than flowers
    Lie still under seaweed and sea!
What lips that have kissed in what bowers!
    What fruits of the tree!

(cont'd., new stanza)

Are they gone, are they vanished forever?
  Are their passions all quenched in the brine?
Must they sleep in a palace and never
  Learn aught of those walls berylline?
Dim grottoes and strewn-over niches
  With amber and opal and pearl —
Is there none to rejoice in those riches,
  No gallant or girl?

Who knows but in caverns of coral,
  Lit round by a lamp not of fire,
They speak in a language not oral
  And love without flesh for desire?
We walk in a world where but cant is
  And measure the motions of Mars —
Who knows but the folk of Atlantis
  Forgive us our stars?

For out of our hearing and vision
  Lie more than our senses can tell —
Fair worlds too minute for division
  And nebulae deeper than Hell.
Thou hast not to do with our seeming
  From the womb to the wave or the sod,
But alone of thy grace is our dreaming,
  Invisible God!

(cont'd., new stanza)

Oh, then, let the eyes of thy lovers
   Grow misty with dreams of thy face
Till the day when thy mercy discovers
   Thy veiled and intolerable grace!
Till the day when the last of the nations,
   From altars of idols bowed down,
Shall arise and with chanted libations
   Hail thee and thy crown!

THE STREETS
BEYOND BAGDAD

I rode, once, through a ruined city's gates,
  Dark with forgotten years and deeds forgotten
And dreams long dead bitter buried hates
  And crumbled roofs and rotten.

The paved ways were grown over green with grass
  And with thick moss the walls were all grown over
And on the great square there was none to pass,
  Nor girl nor laughing lover.

Up, up abandoned stairs I slowly climbed
  By terraces and arched resounding bridges
And domes wherefrom victorious bells had chimed
  Across low roofs and ridges.

The sunset flung a fire on broken stones
  And poured a molten fire through turrets broken,
But in the chill wind there were ghostly tones
  Of ghostly gossip spoken.

(cont'd., new stanza)

"Lo, here," I mused, "there must have lived vain lords,
    Merchants and mountebanks and monks and mages
And kings in gold brocades and graven swords
    And sodomites and sages.

"Here must have revelled men so beautiful
    That women learned the utter dregs of loving,
Wanton and wan through summer nights and cool
    Or down still cloisters roving.

"Here must have been such bodies of young girls
    And such exquisite women's flesh denied them
That men went mad with brushing of bright curls
    And brushing breasts beside them.

"In that deep garden, mystic for the moon,
    What trembling, what triumphant vows were uttered?
What lips were crushed to ecstasies that swoon
    In sobs and madness muttered?

"Who knows, ah, who knows now what stealthy hate
    Crouched in the shadows, patient for a season,
To glean revengeful fruits of delicate
    And amorous tryst and treason?

"And who shall say what pageants in the sun
    Wound in the twisted streets bedimmed with banners?
What captains come from far-off battles won?
    What old-world modes and manners?

(cont'd., new stanza)

"How often rang those echoing martial walls
　　With deafening drums and thunder-throated trumpets!
How was war heralded through ducal halls
　　And o'er strewn beds of strumpets!

"And from what thrones have men been tumbled down?
　　And in what books have men wrought out the story?
What mobs have burned, what heroes held the town?
　　Where is their hoarded glory?"

Whereat I climbed the topmost tower of all,
　　And when the moon rolled up through veils of umber
Then I beheld one standing, mute and tall,
　　Wrapped in a mantle sombre.

"Ah, then," said I, "the city is not dead,
　　Since I have known that one man in his tower
May bind a hungry multitude with dread
　　And break men's hearts with power.

"One man of all who dares and will not yield
　　Shall flaunt out scorn across an audience table
As if he bore Medusa on his shield
　　Or cursed another Babel.

"I wonder Will this figure bear my hail?
　　Or will it vanish like a wraith, I wonder?
And is it man or shall a woman's wail
　　Rive the close night in sunder?"

(cont'd., new stanza)

But even as I watched the woman came
   (For now I saw it was in truth a woman),
Loosing her gathered garment lined with flame,
   Being fair as no thing human.

All naked in the moonlight, like a witch,
   Her long hair, shaken over silver shoulders,
Wove her a wizard's gown embossed and rich
   With art where magic smoulders.

She came and mounted near me and her eyes
   Looked ever through me all the while she mounted,
As one goes mazed in happy histories
   By ancient bards recounted.

Her voice was like a bell, her lifted voice
   Was like a pure bell set to sudden ringing,
For "Mine!" she cried, and cried again, "Rejoice!"
   And echoes answered, singing.

And "Mine! Mine! Mine!" went laughing down the
     streets,
   Cascaded over battlements and hollows,
Like elfin ribaldry some wanderer meets
   And hears and fears and follows.

"Then gradually and yet with gathering speed,
   As if the doomful horns of God had sounded,
Rose people pressing furiously at heed
   From stricken tombs astounded.

(cont'd., new stanza)

Death clanged on broken hinges and the crowd
   Swarmed out upon a city's myriad labors,
While harlots bandied evil, barren browed,
   And boys came beating tabors.

And ladies plumed and booted spurred and sought
   The glance of morioned men on plunging stallions
Caparisoned in or and azure wrought
   With martlets and medallions.

And on the porch of many a temple reared
   To graceful Gods and over all their porches
Went grave priests having mitre and thick beard
   Weird in a gleed of torches.

Then I beheld and lo, there came a king
   To walk with lords by fierce dissension shaken
And give one land and one far voyaging
   And give one captives taken.

But still there rang an echoing through the town
   Where "Mine! Mine! Mine!" repeated and redoubled,
Leaped in an eerie, silvery torrent down
   Dim vaults of years untroubled.

And still "Rejoice!" rolled billowing up and up
   To break along the moon-drenched sands of Heaven
And wash upon the glittering crusted cup
   Held by the Taurian seven.

(cont'd., new stanza)

And now she spoke again and in my ears
    There never shall be silence more — ah, never
Though I am blown beyond all taste of tears
    And all songs else, forever!

"Come unto me and ye shall never die!
    Ye shall not part nor yet be torn in sunder,
For I will hear and I will make reply
    Over all seas and under!

"None knoweth my face, yet I shall never change;
    I am unalterable, I am eternal
Who range through torrid and cold zones and range
    Autumnal worlds and vernal.

"My name goeth forth in thunder in the storm
    And by the choirs of unseen stars is chanted,
My name is Chaos and my name is Form,
    I am death's doom undaunted.

"Come unto me and live! Come unto me,
    O dim with dreams, O glutted men with glory!
I am the maiden mother Mystery!
    I am the human story!"

She cried and gazed and "Mine! Mine! Mine!" again
    Tumbled like gems beyond the city's borders
And flashed across the haunts and homes of men
    And past the pacing warders.

(cont'd., new stanza)

Then stillness. Then a wind before the dawn
   Moaned into haunted palace and pavilion,
Loud with culled leaves and strange with raindrops
     thrown
   Million on muttering million.

And when I looked the ways were grown with grass
   And with thick moss the walls were all grown over
And on the great square there was none to pass,
   Nor girl nor laughing lover.

JUDITH

Surely it is a strange thing now in me,
Who sit all day and ponder on days done,
How my heart beateth on thus endlessly
From noon till each next noontide of the sun,
Seeing that my love hath no more course to run
And my love's feet no ways to wander in
Lest every step be counted, one by one,
  Each for a separate sin.

I, Judith, am a widow in Israel.
Men give me glory, vaunting to my face
That victory over kings and all men tell
Proudly my way of battle in that place
Whereof I take no comfort and no grace,
Being torn in sunder as the people tear
One that hath eaten love's honey in such ways
  As Israel must not share.

I mourn not and I will not mourn again,
Though the stars mourn forever, him whose fame
Rang thunderously among the hills, as when
God's anger belloweth and there falleth flame

(cont'd., no new stanza)

On priest and slave and maid and her that shame
Holdeth in lampless houses all night long,
But will sing — oh beauteously! — his name
    Even in a secret song.

Hear me, ye towns and towers of alien lands!
Where Ashtoreth hath temples and where girls
Reel in delirious dances, having hands
Reddened with roses and mad mouths like merles
For laughter in the sunlight and for pearls
Lashing bare throats and violent bodies bare
And for sweet savors drenching their close curls
    And for love's limbs made fair.

Hear me ye groves and all ye hilltops, hear!
Where mysteries at midnight are being done
For glory of old Gods that still give ear
To the song of the pain and pleasure of flesh made one,
To the sound or the wonder of Tyre and Babylon
And still to the pride which passion gendereth
Riotously in rivers of blood that run
    Deep unto seas of death.

Yea, and ye flowering valleys, hear me now!
For I will sing forever in my heart
A new bright song of triumph, that O thou
Who goest in grave reverence and apart
Shalt have thy spirit move in thee and start
As at, brave horses bearing strong young men
Suddenly down to battle, and as thou art
    Thou shalt not be again.

(cont'd., new stanza)

In the days of famine, even in those days
When Holofernes thronged us round without
In camps of pennoned splendor and the ways
Stormed of the charging chariot and the shout
Of horsemen ranging our wide walls about
And the rumbling trudge of the footmen found our ears,
Then there was thirst, then there were dearth and doubt
    And anger and shame and tears.

In the stark streets the young men and the maids
Fainted and fell, they fainted and fell down dead,
And ancient men sat muttering of cool glades,
And tender women, with dust upon the head,
Sat in their silent doorways, and for dread
The watchers at the gates cursed God and died,
And the high hearts of captains all were sped,
    And there was no more pride.

Then I rose up, even I, and on my feet
Bound sandals and I bound on chains and rings
And garments made for gladness and combed sweet
Spikenard along my hair and delicate things
Of gold put on for girdle and painted wings
Of birds that fly like fire in Eastern lands
And put on gems that had been cut for kings
    And henna upon my hands.

        (cont'd., new stanza)

The eyelids of mine eyes were stained with gold
And red the nipples of my breasts were stained
And silken veils were gathered, fold on fold,
About me and a mystery was gained
With amber-scented bracelets; and I feigned
More than all women after love's desire,
Going mincingly, as if my feet were chained
   As men chain maids in Tyre.

And I went forth and all men looked on me
Marveling and were silent; and I came
Down to the Persian banners, joyously,
Where there were those to halt and have my name —
Such men as ravish women, bearing shame
For that to them none openeth out her feet,
And, evil in the torchlight, eyes of flame
   And mouths not good to meet.

For there had come one to Bethulia
Whose heart was tender even unto this,
That when we met in some secluded way
Where no eye seeth nor any whisper is,
Over my fingers fell his cool swift kiss,
My blood being bitter with long lying by night
Upon a lone bed burdened with dead bliss
   And big with dead delight.

      (cont'd., new stanza)

Yet from a cloud the voice of Achior
Echoed across the distance: "I am come
Peacefully here among you, I that bore,
Even for your safety, their opprobrium
Who are terrible in might and pride therefrom
And who have thrust me forth incontinently,
Wherefore let sound the trumpet and daring drum
   And fight a war with me!"

Then in my heart I said: "I will not fail!"
And unto them made answer: "Take me now
To Holofernes. I will cry him 'Hail!'
And he shall bend the sceptre to my brow,
Seeing that I only can inform him how
Bethulia shall fall, for not by swords
Bethulia shall fall and not by vow
   Of kings or any lords."

High on a bed of cedar and carved gold,
The silks whereof were woven in such wise
As pictured forth love's ways in days of old
And war's old ways and old idolatries,
There, high above the revel of lords and cries
Of wine-drenched throats and peacocks and black
    beasts,
One gazed like God, and there was in his eyes
   A weariness of feasts.

(cont'd., new stanza)

The purple of his raiment burned with gems
Torn from Damascus and the throats of Tyre
And all his captains lolled in diadems
And bracelets of soft gold past all desire.
And who is there to say and who inquire
The value of that spoil of countless camps
Wherein lay fire to kiss the amorous fire
    Of heavy silver lamps?

Men walked on roses and the steaming meats
Were sweet with fallen roses, and the hair
Of all their lovely harlots and the seats
Whereon they sat who sounded cymbals there
Were powdered with blown gold, and everywhere
Went dancers having gold about their cauls,
And fencers and fair boys and eunuchs fair
    And wrestlers who tried falls.

They flayed a captive soldier in that place
So delicately and with exquisite pain
That half his face was torture and half his face
Writhen to curious laughter, and in vain
He called on death to sever the dread chain
Which bindeth ruined body and racked soul
And called on God to grant him but the gain
    Of sleep in swifter dole.

(cont'd., new stanza)

"O wonderful in war, behold thy name
Hath blushed across the world and all men know
How thou art grown and we have heard thy fame
How it hath filled the whole earth, high and low,
Suffer thy servant do thee reverence! Oh,
Suffer me that I serve thy king of kings
With prayer and revelation lest thou go
    Humbled for hidden things!"

"Woman, behold, thy wisdom and thy wit
Move me, and now I see thou hast, also,
Beauty like drum-playing, like the sound of it
Heard in my youth of battles, long ago.
I know there is none like thee and I know
That when those gates are down thou shalt be shod
In shoes of wonder, royally, and lo,
    Thy God shall be my God!

"Eat thou with me and drink and take thine ease,
And if thou wilt have any wealth of mine
Or if thou wilt have all the earth and seas,
They are thine, O bringer of beauty, they are thine!
And if thou wilt but drain one cup of wine
And go again, having said out thy say,
Is there one liveth, mortal or divine,
    Shall bar thy body's way?"

(cont'd., new stanza)

How shall a woman having lips to kiss
And flesh for all the fevers of love's kin
Look upon lechery and furious bliss
Nor long to learn what ease desire may win?
How shall her spirit hear not, then, within,
Those trumpets which, like stallions on the hills,
Neigh their proud song and have no sense of sin
     Nor any fear of ills?

Oh, love in woman is even like as fire
That burneth out the hearts of fallen trees,
Like worms in fruit, leaving the rind entire
But eating at the center, and like these
A love-scored woman standeth with close knees
And calm brows and with mockery on her mouth,
Though her lips ache for kisses and for ease
     Her breasts ache, dry with drouth.

Alas, I might have loved him! For his lips
Drank little wine and little in his life
Cared he for many scented fingertips
And there were few that went with him to wife.
But I remembered and the treacherous knife
Pricked at my breast, being just, and in my heart
God breathed his warning through the silent strife
     And love looked on apart.

(cont'd., new stanza)

Yet in a dream that night he came to me
With conquest in strong arms and body strong
And panting breath that bore tumultuously
From riotous blood burst forth of every thong,
Hurling his muscles on me like a song
Of brutal words flown out on dulcet wings
Or like proud armies entering, throng on throng,
     Through gates of conquered kings.

Oh, give God praise for dreaming in the night!
When women having gentleness and shame
May wallow on deep couches of delight
Nor suffer scandal on a stainless name,
But with wild ways and wanton words of flame
And curious whispers crushed on fervent lips
Drive all life's passion shuddering through the frame,
     Being scourged with soft warm whips.

Give God all praise for dreaming! For alone
In the lewd night thy secret stormy lust
Shall rage across thy body and make moan,
Blinding thy soul with violent gust on gust,
Drenching thy soul with torment and thy dust
Till thou art broken and liest along, the sod
As a flower is broken and in cool earth is thrust —
     Praise ye the Lord thy God!

          (cont'd., new stanza)

But oh, for barren duty unto men
Come quick upon my spirit in that place!
How, now, forever, shall I feel again
His fingers weaving veils of passionate lace
And on my breast his breathing and on my face
The kisses of his mouth and on my thighs
The laboring of his body in love's race
    For love's own mutual prize?

How shall I ever again have pain and pride
In yielding up, on any bridal bed,
All that man seeketh brightly in his bride
For easing of that hunger which hath fed
On fair full flesh that now lieth drained and dead,
Being shorn of charm with pleasure overmuch
When youth goeth sated and all songs are said
    And all joy flown from touch?

For on the fourth night, in his inmost tent,
They made a feast of wine; and unto me
One came with soft words, graciously, being sent
And being returned with soft words, graciously;
Wherefore the lone harp's langorous ecstasy
Throbbed in a muted rhythm and the feet
Of slaves and the hands of slaves went soundlessly
    And the cooled wines were sweet.

      (cont'd., new stanza)

We were alone together and he said
Out of quick love: "O Judith, in thy hair
My soul hath wandered with the unknown dead
And with the unborn had foregathering there.
Where are thy father's images and where
Are thy sons' images to the end of days?
Behold, the beauty of sandals thou dost wear
   Hath led me in strange ways.

"Thy body is like a pool at evening
Whereof the lips of singers have not sung.
Thy body is like warm ivory. I will sing
Unto thy body with a tireless tongue.
Thy body is like a scented censer swung
High in some temple reared to unknown Gods.
I am troubled of all thy body and over flung.
   I am as one scourged with rods.

"How are thy tinted feet like pomegranates
Before a king's face. And thy silken thighs,
How are they bright like some strong city's gates.
And how like mailed men's glory are thine eyes.
Ah, thou art molded in such perfect wise
As the Gods loved a thousand years ago
And thou hast wrung me endlessly with sighs
   And thou art cold like snow.

     (cont'd., new stanza)

"But I would have thee suddenly wake at night
And turn thee unto me in quickening faith
That thou shalt even have thy love's delight
And have thy love's cry stilled between thy breath,
When thy strained limbs and breast that laboreth
And mad mouth moaning under one long kiss
Swoon as within the ultimate arms of death —
    I would have more than this!

"I would that when I go in painted cars
To lead men forth for battle and I would
That when I wearily come from ended wars
In cars gone dull with dust and black with blood,
Yet by that hearth whereon my father stood,
Lord over lords and captain unto kings,
Thee might leave in tears among thy brood
    And find thee rich with rings.

"I know I may not have thee save for love.
I know I may not love thee save forever.
I think eternity hath not years enough
To soothe my sorrow for thee, should we sever.
And if I never gain thy soul and never,
While time floweth on, lose all my being in thee,
Then, quick or dead, I shall be like some river
    That may not find the sea."

(cont'd., new stanza)

O God, thou art more cruel, being just,
Than are young lions in the wilderness!
Thou hast but made man out of utter dust,
Why wilt thou, than thy Sons, condone him less?
Why hast thou given us passion to possess
Man, being woman, and woman, being man?
Why did'st thou question Adam to confess
    That breaking of thy ban?

I said to Holofernes: "Man of earth,
Behold, thy servant hath no will to go
Save in such wise as shall increase thy mirth
And give thee joy of all thy days. For lo,
The years draw on, indifferent and slow,
And in the end of all the hours thereof,
What shall be said of women cold like snow
    More than of them that love?"

Moreover, with low laughter, on my bed
I spread my hair before him and my hands
Wove temptingly before him and I said:
"Thy strength is more than towers in conquered lands.
Who am I, now, that I should bind with bands
Thy rich desire and hold thine arms from me?"
And it was in my throat as if hot sands,
    Being poured, gave agony.

(cont'd., new stanza)

Whereat he called for wine until his heart
Grew merry with much drinking; and the night
Wore old and silent, slowly; and apart
Men passed from ashen watch-fires out of sight;
And when he slept and kept no more of might
And when the last lamp wavered, dull and dim,
Then I rose up and grasped the falchion bright
   And took his head from him.

Strange beyond thought it is and always strange
To watch a strong man's body fallen in death
Where the quiet flesh bath no more will for change
Nor any pleasure more nor pain nor breath,
And strange to learn how passion perisheth
And that which had been thy delight to see
Lieth cold forever, of which no woman saith:
   "This will ease love in me."

I know not how long in the silence there
I watched that warrior's beauty nor what tears
Bathed his pale limbs whereon the close-grown hair
Clung vainly to the jewels about mine ears,
Nor what hours passed before old human fears
Drove me to pull the canopy from the bed
(Ah God! Shall I forget in after years?)
   Wherewith to hide the dead.

(cont'd., new stanza)

But I went forth and through the camp, anon,
No soldier hindering me, and bearing out
That head of Holofernes through the dawn,
Wrapped in gay silks and bundled all about;
And came before the gates; and when the shout
Of the tired warned of lifted spears,
Had not I that to shame a sentry's doubt
    And quiet a sentry's fears?

In the glad streets the young maids and the men
Wantoned for joy, they wantoned and praised God,
And the lean captains roused their hearts up, then,
And got them down and smote as with a rod
All that great headless host; and where they trod
They left but dead men or such men as die
At sunset, lying along the crimson sod,
    And such as lords may buy.

And when the Assyrians had been chased and slain
And when their goods were taken for a spoil,
Then all the men of Israel of the plain
And those that dwelt in mountains left their toil
And fell upon that prey, whereof the moil
Ran through a score of days, and of the stuff
No man so mean but gained much flour and oil
    And honey and wine enough.

        (cont'd., new stanza)

But unto me they brought his crimson tent,
His beds and vessels and his plates of gold,
And all his ivory and his gems they sent
Unto my house, to have and even to hold,
Wherefore my wealth is as a tale untold
And no man in Bethulia, seeing me,
But saith in his heart: "Though thou wert old
    Yet would I mate with thee."

And Achior the Ammonite fell down
And reverenced me and would have kissed my hands
Even in the sight of the assembled town,
And all the laughing women made out bands
For dancing and for waving of green wands,
And there went riders out of every gate
To blow my glory over wondering lands
    And make mine honor great.

Wherefore I give God praise and will rejoice
With harps and timbrels. As for Achior,
Let him have all fair women of his choice
So he come not again unto my door.
For I will live as I have lived before,
I, Judith, being a widow in Israel,
And that which hath been shall be done no more
    Forever. And it is well.

(cont'd., new stanza)

Thus I come crowned with victory to my kin.
My name goeth on before all men. And yet
I am as one damned utterly for sin,
I am a whore bowed down to my regret.
Where shall I hide my fame and where forget
The evil of mine honor? In what wine
Shall I drown memory of the shameful sweat
    Of virtue that was mine?

How shall I care for glory and for praise
From other men, who have of mine own will
Put from me that which till the end of days
Were sweeter though but cursing? How fulfill
The lineage of my fathers or instill
In my sons' hearts desire for duty done?
Still m mine ears that lie must burn and still
    While stars fall, one by one.

But surely there are vales in infinite space
Where the stern God shall never come and where
Two souls may rest, abandoned of his face
And lost to toil and truth and duty there.
Surely there is some realm devoid of care,
Some cycle of pure joy wherein desire
Hath not to pander unto faith and wear
    The livery of a liar.

                (cont'd., new stanza)

Thus I will sing, even in mine inmost heart,
A new bright song of triumph, beauteously,
That O thou Holofernes, where thou art
Thou shalt not long with vain desire for me!
Over the mountains and the barren sea,
Out of the grave, for all its bolts and bars,
Oh, I will follow, I will follow thee
    Beyond the eternal stars!

Beyond the stars together and beyond
The moonlight and the sunlight and all gaze
Of men and angels of whom God is fond
Because they lift up song to him and praise,
Oh, out where love hath justice of his days,
Room for his wings and for his dreaming room
And for his peace and freedom from all old ways
    And freedom for his own doom.

And if it be that after countless years
Thou, looking on the essence of my worth,
Art sad within thy spirit more than tears
Or any sign of sorrow endured on earth,
Then if thou wilt have fellows for thy mirth,
Creeds for thy faith and all the care thereof,
Let it be cried to the utter bounds of birth:
    "Not God hath failed, but love!"

BATHSHEBA

I have been summoned; I have seen the king;
And he hath granted all my long desire.
He lieth upon his bed of sorrowing
With lank and matted locks and mouth like mire;
And there one twangleth ever at a wire
And round about are divers tongues to wag;
But cold he lieth for all the hovering fire
    Of maiden Abishag.

God knoweth her fairer now than any of us
In even our good days gone! But what hath she?
The wreck and ruin of one once valorous
Who cannot break her vain virginity!
Oh, let her glean from wan eyes watery
Love's leavings and from stiffening, waxen lips
An old man's kiss, enduring patiently
    An old man's fingertips!

I wonder would she marvel, could she know
What I have known of David in the days
When forth he rode to battle, long ago,
In gold and crimson and with shield ablaze.

(cont'd., no new stanza)

How thronged the press of people, mouthing praise!
How chariots thundered, car on glittering car,
With storms of stallions darkening down the ways
    The king marked out for war!

It was no blinkard maunderer that came
Upon the house-tops in the evening light
While yet the day's wide window burned with flame
Poured gloriously along the hills of night;
The man that watched me make my body white
Stood strong athwart his kingdom and his pride
Recked not of God for sufferance nor his might
    Of man for choice of bride!

He sent for me and took me. Glad with gold
His great hands broke that other's hold of me,
Howbeit Uriah's heart beat high and bold,
Nor would he fawn nor bend a warrior's knee,
But walked undaunted on his destiny —
Sometimes I wake at night and think of him,
A plain, brave man to merit honestly
    The welcoming Seraphim.

And I remember-how shall I forget? —
When David's house was bare and men would come
From costly courts ambassadors and set
Their gifts before the wild Prince Absalom,
And how the King smiled ever and was dumb
Or, musing over caskets rich with nard,
Lifted his great head suddenly to the drum
    Where Joab changed the guard.

(cont'd., new stanza)

There lay no leopards in the garden, then,
Nor many women; and the king in hall
Moved as a warrior moves among his men
When there is equity between them all;
Yet I have seen him quell a drunken brawl,
Striding like doom among the thrusting blades,
As might a sunbeam thrown beyond a wall
   Dispel the gathered shades.

And in those days there was a man to lie
Upon a hard bed strewn along the floor,
But sweeter for deep slumber than the high
And perfumed couch that youth shall press no more
And sweeter, ah, God! sweeter for love's lore
And all the secret works and words of love
Than ever man and woman shared before
   Or ever dreamed thereof.

Oh, God, my youth gone from me! Oh, the days
When life was pleasant on my lips and tongue,
The lordly banquets ringing round with praise,
The harps were sounded and the songs were sung,
The beauty of women, oh, like banners flung
Silken and splendid over marching men,
The lays, the lips, the loves when I was young
   Who shall not love again!

      (cont'd., new stanza)

Oh, flesh that I have fondled! Fingertips
That burned me over like small tongues of fire!
Oh, cruel kisses bitten through love's lips!
Oh, tears wrung deep from labor of desire!
Oh, bitter, brief, bright ecstasies that tire
Or ever their words are said between love's breath!
Oh, roses fallen from a smoldering pyre!
    Oh, gold rings damned with death!

And think not that for Nathan's anger I
Could ever scourge my spirit to regret.
Though I had borne a score of babes to die
In mockery of tears and bearing sweat,
Yet had I been not less the queen and yet
Not less the mother of a race of kings
Then mated basely with a clown to get
    And breed up underlings.

For Solomon shall reign, my son shall reign!
The King hath heard my prayer and he hath sworn.
And men are fled apart and Joab slain
And Adonijah taken on the Horn.
Ye women! Witness ye that I have borne
A king, that I have borne a king to be
A glory unto Israel and adorn
    Her God's house royally.

(cont'd., new stanza)

And I shall walk in scarlet and my feet
Shall be shod on with leather and my hair
Bound up with snakes of ivory made to meet
And mate with amber serpents twisted there.
Bleeding with rubies, I will work and wear
Soft silks burned over with such priceless gems
As only women of a king may tear
    From conquered diadems.

The purple hearts of sapphires and the eyes
Of topaz I will have and all my girls
Shall gleam for bearing thick on breasts and thighs
Those embers that are opals and for pearls
Wept out of Heaven, long ago, where curls
The lone South Sea to isles of amethyst
And emeralds more lovely than the whorls
    Of young leaves rimmed with mist.

Dwellers in tents, the desert tribes shall come
With fleeces whiter than a maiden's feet;
The Mede shall march with cymbal and with drum,
The Scythian hordes with barley and fine wheat;
And Tyre shall trade and Sidon end and treat
And heathen nations from beyond the seas
Shall give thick gold and all rare things and sweet
    And all things good for ease.

(cont'd., new stanza)

The cities of the world shall comfort thee,
O Israel! And all its laboring ships
Shall bear their burdens to thy treasury
And thou shalt be as one who sits and sips
Honey and wine made cool with snow that drips
From dark deep hollows in the tumbled hills
And thou shalt have sweet savors at thy lips
    And no more taste of ills.

Thou shalt go mailed in silver and thy shield
Shall be of beaten burnished plates of gold;
The color of thy kings' tents pitched in field
Shall be of Tyrian purple. Who shall hold
Triumphantly against thee, as of old?
And who shall bear the shaking of thy spear?
Thy days have not been numbered nor been told
    The deeds that thou shalt hear.

For lo, now, God hath raised a young man up
To judge thee and to weld thy tribes in one;
And thou shalt eat with justice and thy cup
Shall brim with mercy under Solomon;
And all that live and move beneath the sun
Shall know thee what thou art; and every clime
Shall praise thee; and the lords of Babylon
    Shall fear thee out of time.

        (cont'd., new stanza)

There never shall be any more at all
Forgetfulness of thee forever; thou
Shalt be a deathless beauty mystical
In woven veils of temples; on thy brow
The morning star shall flame, as even now
Till Eden be re-opened and the bar
Against thy sins and sufferings allow
    Peace and the evening star.

MICHAL

I am the childless woman. I am she
That is a king's daughter, being seed of Saul.
My beauty hath fallen upon me and broken me
And I am become as one for whom men call,
Muttering each to other: "Is this all?
Hath the last word to say been sometime said?"
Wherefore my days are bitter for drained gall
　　And all my joy is dead.

How long ago it seemeth since this King
Came, beautiful with battle, down the street
Where women danced in joy of song-singing,
"Lo, Saul hath slain his thousands!" (And most meet)
"But David his ten thousands!" Yet how sweet,
Even now, the memory of my pride in him
Whose hair was as the waving of long wheat
　　By wings of Cherubim.

It is not well with maidens having pride
If love lay heavy longing over them,
Seeing that before love's mercy shall have died
Scorn weareth again his ancient diadem.

(cont'd., no new stanza)

148

Let her sew ever at some virgin hem
Who hath not quick forgiveness for men's deeds
And Crush love's rose and cast the proffered stem
    To wither among weeds.

I am come down from heroes in the hills.
The women of my tribe are strong and proud.
Not for hopes broken nor for future ills
Will they sit brooding at the fire and bowed,
But, calm before the vulgar wondering crowd,
Will walk with high heads, having death at heart,
Yea, as that Ruth, serene and golden-browed,
    Who would not turn and part.

Wherefore it were a meet thing that our love
Had ridden over all proud words of ours,
Gaining great sons to follow us, whereof
Our blood had been like walls and like strong towers
Reared on the hills and beautiful with flowers,
Being long unbeaten by wide waves of war,
And daughters born to bear bright kings for dowers
    In farther lands and far.

For I that was the first of David's loves,
Gained with a double tale of warriors dead,
How could I put away, like outworn gloves,
Our swooning kisses and the songs we said?
How could I banish out of Phalti's bed
The body of one whose lips were on my tears,
The beauty of one like fire about my head
    Through all those loveless years?

(cont'd., new stanza)

But when I saw him dancing through the town
Like any common soldier, in my heart
I said: "Behold, thy hero playeth the clown
And as a widowed woman, now, thou art.
Nay, let not from thine eyes the tears outstart
Nor memory of lone nights upon thy bed
Pierce thee with passion sharper than the dart
    Of scorn that thou hast said."

I am the childless woman. Look on me,
Ye mothers and ye boasters of babes borne.
I am the childless woman. Shall ye see
Such as I am, again, for all your scorn?
I am the childless woman. Go, adorn
Your bodies with the spoils of Babylon's kings,
And shall your beauty be as mine when shorn
    Even of my finger rings?

Behold, I am a javelin and a sword.
I am swift steel that beareth base men down
And all base worship of that unknown Lord
Who dwelleth nor in tents nor any town.
I am the glory of princes and the crown,
Being big with learning over common men.
I am the childless woman that no clown
    Shall dare to love again.

Ye mothers and ye boasters! Dare ye send
Sons of your servile bodies down all time?
But they shall hold me greater in the end,
Who loved less folly in my King than crime.

(cont'd., no new stanza)

Yea, for the bright day cometh wherein each clime
Shall breed men better than to leap and dance,
Drunk with God-madness as some sorry mime
    Goeth drunk with wine, perchance.

I am the childless woman. But had I
Borne a man child to reign in Israel,
Behold, I had shown him deeper down the sky
Than fair fenced Heaven and fenced fantastic Hell.
I had taught well my son it is not well
When kings bow down to sowers' and gleaners' Gods,
Since no man knoweth of truth nor can one tell
    What lieth beyond the sods.

Ye know me and ye fear me and ye hate
For that I have dared more than any of you,
O babblers and poor fawners upon fate,
O cowardly of heart that still pursue
The failing ghost of life and lift up hue,
But who, being tired, would fain be taken of death,
Save that ye dare not, save that ye must do
    The toil of blood and breath.

Wherefores because my father parted me
From David in the years when we were young,
All men forever shall mourn me bitterly
And mourn with me the songs he might have sung,
All delicate vain men that rung by rung
Climb up towards God on ladders of pure art,
Each man knowing well God hath no way among
    The faiths are in man's heart.

(cont'd., new stanza)

Over the wide world they shall hear of me
And, hearing, shall remember me and say:
"This woman's eyes were colder than the sea
And haughtier than the hills, this woman's way."
And they shall give me honor in that day,
Having no longer any Gods to kiss
With pale lips fearful of the night, and they
    Shall have much joy of this.

But now I lie alone along my bed
Who have put by youth and put by lecheries,
Being as one banished, even as one fled
Out of all lands and over long, dark seas.
I am a childless woman without ease,
Yet do I weep not nor will I implore.
I have my pride, I have my memories!
    What have ye boasters more?

ABISHAG

(A Double Sestina)

If any man have pity upon me
When I am dead hereafter, let him say:
"This woman's days were all one bitterness
For that, or ere love laughed, lo, love lay dead."
And when men go in swift ships oversea
Unto bright isles where it is always day
Beyond all nations that wise men may guess
And whence all sorrow and tears are long time fled,
Let them bear tidings of me, bitterly,
And speak sad words of me along their way,
That all fair women having mouths to press
May mourn in pity of my loveless bed.

God knoweth I took no joy of David's bed,
Whose body hungered after heat from me,
Nor aught of gladness for a king to press
Wan lips on lips that had no love to say,
But, silent after every woman's way,
Endured a brief while in all bitterness
With bright low laughter breaking bitterly
From broken dreams whereof the pride lay dead.

(cont'd., no new stanza)

153

For being wife with maiden fancies fled,
Oh, farther fled than ships gone down to sea,
How could I know of love's days, then, or guess
That in love's land it might be always day?

Yet only love bath tears beyond his day,
Since all griefs else are banished at love's bed.
Wherefore, being widowed, could I know or guess
That laughing women might not make for me
Soft linen whiter than white foam of sea,
Whereon my true love's body might well press
Till all the swift sweet hours of night were fled
And there were no more sweet swift words to say?
But only on my grave, when I am dead,
Shall there be roses laid in bridal way
To deck death's marriage with me, bitterly,
After this burden of much bitterness.

Oh, low light lutes played after bitterness
When love and I, on all a summer's day,
Forgot to hear the wise world bitterly
Mourning for sorrow on a lonely bed,
But laughed and loitered down a secret way
Whereon were strange wild roses good to guess,
Till days gone over were become as dead
And pride of passion burned again in me,
Knowing more beauty than all life could say
Because the tides of it were as the sea
Which followed ever after moons that fled
Like maidens having fruitful mouths to press.

(cont'd., new stanza)

How shall it be when other men shall press
Swift kisses on my body's bitterness?
And shall it be that all desire bath fled,
Yea, gone with love forever and a day?
Or shall it be that life prove like the sea
Now singing and now sobbing bitterly?
For only of things past can wise men say
And no man knoweth if he shall rise from bed,
Having lain down thereon. Can youth in me
Keep any more remembrance of love's way
Before my youth's eyes looked upon love dead?
Hath love one life or many? Who can guess?

Ah love, ah love! Had there been one to guess
That nevermore forever should I press
My lips along his temples that is dead
Beyond all memories of old bitterness!
Had there been one to meet us in the way
Or ever our dear days of dalliance fled,
Ah, surely he had hearkened unto me,
Being sad for beauty overmuch that day,
And we had passed afar and made our bed
In some bright isle across the unknown sea
Where no man might have majesty to say
Dread doom of death in anger, bitterly!

Ah love, thou art more cruel, bitterly,
Than man or any woman may well guess
When thou hast only half thy words to say
With kisses that but one alone will press,
Wherefore thy glory, like the savage sea,

(cont'd., no new stanza)

Feedeth on broken beauty and men dead
And tears more salt for sadness on thy bed
Than are the salt sea's waves with bitterness.
And thou hast more desire to live thy day
When there is none to welcome thy wild way
Than did my true love hunger after me,
Knowing I but feigned to flee him when I fled.

Yet wherefore now should any more be fled
Or welcome love or love come bitterly?
Since joy will not be ever unto me
Save in such wise as old men seek to guess,
When I shall have put by this fair warm way
In lands whereof not even wise men say
More than in those lands it is always day.
And wherefore, also, if some king will press
Lips from which cometh only bitterness,
Should I have more of sorrow than the sea
That hath had many men unto her bed
Who are gone, who are vanished, being long time dead?

All things are well with women and men dead
For whom desire is done and sorrow fled,
Where, drowned in deeper darkness than the sea,
They sleep inviolate on their dreamless bed.
All things are over that bear bitterly
On men and on quick women and on me.

(cont'd., no new stanza)

For well God knoweth how more of bitterness
There is than pleasure in this human way
Whereon none hath his utmost will to press
Love's lips or ever death, when none may guess,
Beareth him swiftly out of time and day
With all his songs to sing, his words to say.

I know not any more what words to say,
Being born to will that I were only dead,
Broken in dust and blown beyond the day
Where all forgotten things are long time fled.
For what man shall have profit who will guess
Sorrow bath any end gave bitterly
Down in the bitter grave in such foul way
As no quick man that tosseth on his bed
Would have the fairest woman's mouth to press,
Nay, nor the king to crush one kiss from me,
Though it were yielded without bitterness
And though my lips held mystery as the sea?

Nor can I think that life is as the sea
Whereof men say there is no end and say
That only on this shore is bitterness
And that they put by sorrow who are fled.
Ah God, ah God! Have pity upon me!
I am but one who wandereth all at guess
Between two days whereof one day is dead
And dead to me shall be that other day.
I am but one who crieth bitterly,
Having no comfort though I plead and press
My weary eyes to find thee from my bed
And my tired feet to follow in thy way.

(cont'd., new stanza)

Thus, love, I will remember in what way
I walked aforetime, singing by the sea,
Seeking what flowers to gather for my bed
To charm thee out of all thy bitterness.
I will forget my sorrows, bitterly,
With dreaming how thy laughter is not fled
And dreaming that I still can hear thee say
Thine arms will hold me and thy kisses press
Long after the unchanging stars are dead
And when not any man hath cause to guess
What lieth beyond the utter end of day —
Ah love, I will remember! Comfort me!

Go bitterly, my song, and make thy way.
Live thy one day flown out beyond the sea.
How can I guess, for sorrow upon my bed,
What, of one fled, men shall hereafter say
When bitterness hath vanished out of me
Who have to press no quick lips more, being dead?

A SONG OF
SOLOMON

The Queen she came in a golden chair,
　　In a golden chair all out of the South,
With bands of amber binding her hair
　　And lips that longed for a kingly mouth,
And all the feet of her dancing-girls
　　Came shod with purple for men's delight,
And, all in ebony, priceless pearls
　　And cups and opals and armor bright.

The King he rose from his throne and then
　　He looked to the left, he looked to the right
Where apes and ivory, warlike men,
　　Leopards and peacocks ranged in sight,
And he said: "Behold, it is given to thee,
　　All thy desire of all things mine.
Ask and be granted! Ask of me
　　Half of the kingdom, lo, 'is thine!"

"O King, I come from a land of spice
　　Pleasant with perfume, flowing with milk,

(cont'd., no new stanza)

Where men came riding in rare device
    Of silver working on cloaks of silk.
And I said in my heart: 'I will get me up
    To the boasted court of this King and laugh!'
(For so I said to my secret cup).
    But half was not told to me, no, not half!"

"O Queen, the words of thy mouth are sweet!"
    "O King, the words of thy mouth are wise
And happy the lips that kiss thy feet!"
    "Thrice happy the lips that kiss thine eyes!"
"I will bid them sing in my fathers' halls
    Only thy glory and sounding name!"
"And I will grave on the temple's walls
    Tales of thy beauty in gold and flame!"

So the King he seated beside him there
    That fair young Queen come out of the South
And he murmured over her hands and hair,
    "Kiss me with kisses of thy mouth!"
And the Queen she dwelt for a year and a day
    And all her desire he gave to her
And a thousand servants to smooth her way
    With roses and cinnamon, oil and myrrh.

But a fool that lived at the court of the King,
    Evil with envy, bitter with lust,
Was wont to twangle a harp and sing,
    "Passion and splendor — death and dust!"
And when the day of their love was done
    This fool waxed great in the minds of men.
But the King grew weary under the sun.
    And the Queen went into the South again.

THE WANDERER

The sands were bright, like crumbled gold,
Along the road to Ispahan;
The noons were hot, the nights were cold,
There was no ease for beast or man;
But where the pleasant streams began
To lead by gardens cool and dim,
He saw in soul the deep divan
    Whereon one waited him.

Then he remembered blazing lamps
That burned the perfumed nights away
And doors that barred with iron clamps
Maidens and long lean beasts of prey
And myriad mantles grave and gay
Wherein men's forms and women's forms
Lusted for Caesar's lips to say,
    "Let death be loosed in storms!"

Slaves of the North and Nubian slaves
That led great cats by chains of steel
Writhen in roses . . . wolves in waves . . .
A man bound on some chariot wheel . . .

(cont'd., no new stanza)

Girls ravished there and made to feel
Shame to the last least lingering breath . . .
Harlots . . . and Vestals that must reel,
　　Being dizzy and drunk with death.

And he remembered halls and kings
Who therein feasted languid lords
That looked unmoved at hideous things —
Young boys flayed wantonly with cords,
Young maids divided with dull swords —
To rouse the ruined hearts of queens;
And he remembered afterwards
　　A pleasure in such scenes.

There grew a vision in his eyes
Of orgies where the Queen of Love
Reigned in her temple in some wise
Like sin and all the brood thereof
And in some wise serene above
The pride and petty pains of men,
Being Goddess and being stern to prove
　　Jove's will in all things, then.

And he beheld the sack of towns
Where all the walls went rank and red
And captains gathered high renowns
While madmen marred the wordless dead,
And he beheld what tears were shed
And how the winds were wild with flame
And how the world went sick with dread
　　And Heaven went sick with shame.

(cont'd., new stanza)

And thus he rode by golden sands
To where the pleasant streams began
That watered all the garden-lands
Beneath the walls of Ispahan.
And thus he rode and always ran
His violent vision, gaunt and grim,
To one that on a deep divan
    Waited and watched for him.

BLACK MARGOT

Black Margot walks at midnight
    And one there is to meet;
For lovers must lie lightly
    While lovers' lips are sweet.

His arm goeth well around her,
    And who is there to know?
And who is there to tell, now,
    Aught of Black Margot?

Of all the stars in Heaven
    The pool hath one to show,
Black Margot loveth none other man,
    None other Black Margot.

And there bath come a merchant
    Out of a far town
And brought his one fair daughter
    In a purple gown.

(cont'd., new stanza)

And she hath gone at noontide
  In a gown of silken green
And heard the young men whisper,
  Walking there between.

And she hath gone at twilight
  Loitering down the lane.
But oh, for those that wander
  And come not home again!

And there hath gone a merchant
  Unto a far town
And left his one fair daughter
  In a golden gown.

In a golden gown he left her
  And she hath candles whole
And many a mass there is to say
  For saving of her soul.

One knife, one knife between them!
  And who was there to know
And who was there to whisper
  Word of Black Margot?

But lovers must lie lightly —
  O Son of Mary, save!
Black Margot walks at midnight
  Out of a crossroads grave.

DAUGHTERS OF JOY

Since youth is gone and beauty all gone over
   And no man any more comes in to kiss,
   Now let us leave this house where pleasure is
And, going with brave music, like a lover,
Fare forth where there are flowers and green clover
   And bright hills bending to the sea's long breast,
And for a brief while play the radiant rover
   And, after roving, rest.

Let us forego the evil arms, the faces
   That are as one face evil with desire,
   The broken men, the souls burned out entire
In many a gay girl's passionless embraces,
And having put off silks and scented laces
   And having put cool garments on and white,
Let us go forth and find out quiet places
   And find the still, dark night.

There must be whispering things in virgin grasses,
   In whispering leaves there must be virgin things,
   And somewhere love that labors and yet sings
And love that weeps in sorrow when it passes.

(cont'd., no new stanza)

166

Oh, let's go drink of stronger wine from glasses
  Deeper than ever shame has bubbled in
And look on lads unjaded yet with lasses
  And men not sick with sin.

Daughters of joy, we have trod out our measure,
  We are grown tired and we are growing old.
  Surely we gave for silver and for gold
Something of good, some petty part of pleasure,
Surely we may go now and have our leisure
  On dim beds, and a little time for tears,
Who have laughed long and gained so little treasure
  And toiled so many years.

We are a sisterhood forgot, forsaken.
  Where are our lovers now, where are they gone?
  Shall we rise up and greet them in the dawn,
As men and beautiful proud women waken?
But we have tarried, we are overtaken
  And overshadowed by oblivion's wings.
Weep and remember! But what hearts are shaken
  With pity of outworn things?

Alas, the days of gladness and rich wages
  When we went gowned in beauty and shod with pride!
  Alas, for heavy hair and bosoms dyed
With rubies and rare gems wherein flame rages!
Alas, for laughing lovers and sad sages
  And beautiful cold saints in whom to rouse
Older desires than chaste come down the ages!
  Alas, the ruined house!

(cont'd., new stanza)

Oh, we shall miss the revels and the roses,
 Bright envy and dark faith and bitter hate;
 We shall not learn contentment, though so late,
Nor learn repose, as all old age reposes;
We shall look back, lament, and in brief dozes
 Dream and be grieved with dreaming of things done.
Weep and remember ere the grave's door closes
 Between us and the sun!

And where we labored other girls shall follow,
 Reckless and young and having scorn of us
 And clean swift feet and faces glorious
And wild souls winged for lightness as the swallow,
And they shall wallow in thick lust and wallow
 In deep soft beds, and at the end thereof
Shall they not mourn all dead desires and hollow
 As all we mourn dead love?

Let us go now, being done with all endeavor,
 And go beyond the city and find rest.
 We are too old for beauty. We were best
Away, gone down, forgotten, brought to sever.
We shall not dance for joy again and never
 Shall we fling fire from fingers tremulous,
But we shall lie in the dull grave forever —
 Mary, have mercy on us!

DISAVOWAL

Where will you go when our parting is over?
   Into the wilderness? Into the town?
Will you be glad for a commonplace lover
   Or wait for a man of some pride and renown?
Will you remember me, then, and be bitter,
   Speaking my name with a little wry smile
Or will you forget and agree with a titter
   It was worth while?

Once we were strangers and what did it matter
   When in the night we awakened, alone,
Hearing the dull, the interminable patter
   Of rain on the roofs and of rain over stone?
What could it mean to one, then, if the other
   Might be in trouble, in travail, in tears?
But now shall we ever be able to smother
   That doubt through the years?

Parted with smiles and with pressure of fingers,
   Parted with one little look in the eyes,
Parted with heartbreak and heartbreak that lingers,
   Parted with passion bowed down to the wise,

(cont'd., no new stanza)

Parted with perfume of kisses that never,
   While love is delight and desire in the heart,
Shall fade away — fade away! — oh, that forever
   Must live and must part!

This is the wages of kisses and laughter,
   Man shall grow weary and woman grow wan,
Yet to the grave and it may be thereafter
   There'll be regard for the things that are gone.
There shall be spectres to mock and to mutter:
   "Ah, but it might have been different with you
If only that least little taint of the gutter
   Had not broken through!"

Nothing can end though the body be broken,
   Nothing can cease though the soul disappear;
The songs that were sung and the words that were
     spoken
   Somewhere must echo though all's empty here.
There is but one kind of force in the ether,
   Who, then, shall add to it, who, then, destroy?
Not the sad mourners, the barren ones, neither
   The bringers of joy.

I will go forth to some singer's adventure,
   Eager for honor or bitter for blame,
Cursing, it may be, the laws that indenture,
   The creeds that deform and the crowds that defame,
I will go forth and forget you forever,
   Laugh and forget you — but living or dead,
I'll never sing quite as I have sung and never
   Say as I've said.

(cont'd., new stanza)

Deep roll the waves over deathless Atlantis,
    Deep roll the waves over temple and dome,
But the prayer that we utter, the song that we chant is
    Come down unchanged from that long-buried home.
Deep roll the waves, and the world they befriended
    Heeds them no more, neither lauds them with me,
But their toil is not lost and their glory not ended,
    Nor ever shall be.

All that a man shall have hope of in Heaven,
    All that a woman have help of in Hell
Burns in the need of a strength that has striven
    To endure as a wave in the sound of a bell.
Though the infinite endless result shall be hidden
    From men lying deep in thick dungeons of years,
Shall the surge and the sound unto one be forbidden
    Who hears as God hears?

Nothing shall pass and be silent and vanish
    Into oblivion, once it has been,
Nor shall one banish meek virtue nor banish
    The pride and the pomp and the passion of sin.
Love shall remain and the pleasure of evil,
    Hope shall not end nor the beauty of hate,
And sorrow and labor and song and the devil
    Shall not abate.

Endlessly, endlessly all things of wonder
    Out of the dark Imperceptible flow
Through ripples of light and through billows of thunder
    And into the dark Imperceptible go.

(cont'd., no new stanza)

Ah, the inscrutable face of that Mystery!
   Ah, the inflexible soul of that Sphinx
Whose lip never utters one sentence of history,
   Whose eye never blinks!

This is the Absolute, this the Eternal,
   This, then, is God of the infinite scheme,
In whom there is naught of divine nor infernal
   Nor aught of desire nor the need of a dream.
Ah, where is Jupiter, kindly All-Father,
   Maker of worlds to a plain, simple plan?
Whose face was not madness to look on but, rather,
   A mercy to man.

Ah, where is Moloch, the cruel, the sateless,
   Burner of babes and the Ammonites' pride?
There was a God! Where is Yahveh, the mateless
   Sire of a Son who was human and died?
Where is old Odin, that scorner of ocean?
   Wide were the ways of his warriors in ships!
And the virgin Selene who swooned out emotion
   On sleep-summoned lips?

Now they are gone away, gone away, shaken
   Down from their thrones on the hills of the world,
Exiled and gone and their places are taken,
   Their places are taken from which they were hurled!
Where — for naught perishes — where is that beauty
   Wrought by the old understandable Gods?
And the love of delight and the dower of duty
   For kings and for clods?

(cont'd., new stanza)

What have we gained by the false Gods' dethroning?
  What are we given and what do we gain?
Shame for disorder, contempt for condoning,
  Scorn for ambition and pity for pain.
What can we dare now in manner whole-hearted?
  How live again in a fool's Paradise
With feasting for birth and with tears for the parted
  And wine for the wise?

Let us go hence when our parting is over,
  One to the sunset and one to the dawn,
We have eaten the honey and lain in the clover,
  Now it is over, come, let us be gone!
For love that we worshipped with many libations
  Is broken, is banished and reigns in his room
One perfect, implacable, hailed of the nations,
  A doer of doom.

If we had died in the days of our passion,
  Were it not better than living to learn
Naught shall endure that a mortal may fashion,
  Naught pass away that a God may discern?
Change is our tragedy, change in the Timeless,
  Time is our comedy, timeless in change,
And the theme of our acting is reasonless, rhymeless
  And endless and strange.

(cont'd., new stanza)

Let us go hence and leave God to remember,
  Let us go hence and leave God to explain.
He holds the fire that has gone from the ember,
    His is the soul that has passed out of pain.
Only, we know, that if former and latter
Merge not as one thing with even and odd,
Death is not living. And what shall it matter?
  Leave it to God.

PART FOUR

Why should we fear to have done with fretting
At lust and labor and hate and play?
Death is only a long forgetting
After the sundown, hidden away.

BALLADE TO THE PURITANS

Hear me now for my good lay,
O canting Pharisees and cheating!
It is meet that men should pray,
Since that life is frail and fleeting,
Yet on shining days and sleeting,
Lest ye lose the human touch,
Joy in drinking and in eating —
Be not righteous overmuch.

Dance while yet the time is May,
Forms are fair and hearts are beating,
When the Piper claims his pay
Turn ye then from swain and sweeting.
Soon, beside the fire, entreating,
Hands grown old shall claw and clutch
All in vain for youth's completing —
Be not righteous overmuch.

(cont'd., new stanza)

"Drink no longer water" — yea,
These be words that bear repeating!
"Drink no longer water." — nay,
Once in Cana there was treating
With a glorious wine and heating
To a board of saints and such,
Bridal toast and merry greeting —
Be not righteous overmuch.

L'ENVOI

From the grave there's no retreating,
   Death guards well the wormy hutch,
   Never parting more nor meeting —
   Be not righteous overmuch!

BALLADE OF MUTABILITY

Behold, thou art fair, my love, behold, thou art fair,
Like as one loved of old by Solomon;
Thou hast doves' eyes within thy locks; thy hair
Is pleasant as a stream from Lebanon;
Sweeter than calamus and cinnamon
Thy mouth; thy breast is whiter than white flame;
But — yet a day! — thy beauty shall be done
And time shall be when thou art but a name.

And wilt thou seek out Lesbos, then, and there
Rear up a tower of music toward the sun,
Where all day long run purple seas and where
The nights are nard for memories halcyon?
Where, Sappho, thy pure songs, from passion spun,
Must break men's hearts, but Lesbian waves proclaim
Thy tower shall fall, yea, even as Babylon,
And time shall be when thou art but a name.

(cont'd., new stanza)

All hail, victorious Soldier, hail! The blare
Of brazen bugles vaunting battles won,
The pageantry, the revelry, the prayer
In all the pomps of glory's orison,
And echoes wild of war, as gun on gun
Thunders thy welcome and thy sounding fame —
"Remember thou art mortal," whispers one,
"And time shall be when thou art but a name!"

L'ENVOI

Prince, there is none more loved of honor, none;
Thy deeds are blazoned which renown shall claim;
But Caesar dares no more the Rubicon,
And time shall be when thou art but a name.

BALLADE OF TWO LADIES

Ah, Circe, in your golden isle
Above the golden Grecian sea,
I learned the marvel of your smile,
Your beauty broke the heart of me.
Sweet were your eyes with mystery
And your white body sweet to kiss.
Alas, that we must parted be! . . .
(I wonder where Calypso is.)

Enchantress! Though the world revile
Your acts, your arts, your perfidy,
Could I condemn or blame you while
Your beauty broke the heart of me?
Fair hair and blown that wantonly
The sea-wind's fingers twined in his
Far from the good Penelope . . .
(I wonder where Calypso is.)

(cont'd., new stanza)

181

Your love has mile on weary mile
Beguiled my toil with witchery,
Your songs my day-dreams yet beguile,
Your beauty broke the heart of me.
No more forever, now, shall we —
We two, regain those hours of bliss
In life nor all eternity! . . .
(I wonder where Calypso is.)

L'ENVOI

When age her weird of years shall dree,
Remember, oh, remember this —
Your beauty broke the heart of me! . . .
(I wonder where Calypso is.)

BALLADE OF MAN'S LAST NEED

A pickaxe and a spade

— Sir Thomas Wyatt.

Not silver, no nor gold
Nor silken banners blent
Nor any pomps of old
Along the ways they went
Might in the end prevent,
Nor might the tested blade —
On these their prayers were bent:
A pickaxe and a spade.

How have men thought to hold
High place and government
Who came to have the mould
Drawn round them as a tent!
How have rare dreams been shent!
What loves have looked, dismayed,
On hands that coldly hent
A pickaxe and a spade!

(cont'd., new stanza)

Louder than drums that rolled,
More soft than manners gent,
As trite as tales twice told,
Futile as argument —
All songs the Gods have lent,
All tunes by fingers played
Echo, like money spent,
"A pickaxe and a spade."

L'ENVOI

Lady, when I am pent
Where all dead men are laid,
Have, of your mercy, sent
A pickaxe and a spade!

BALLADE IN TIME
OF THE
GREAT WAR

Reign of ruin! Who rides by night
Over the roads and past the weirs?
Looms a troop in the lurid light,
Rings a cry on the startled ears,
Hoof-beats volley among the meers,
The winds rush down and the dead leaves dance —
Rapiers, rapiers! Musketeers
Ride again in the land of France!

Boots and saddles! And bold and bright
Youth goes galloping, youth that jeers
Death and the dust in pride of might —
War is ever the word it hears;
Peace is ever the pact it fears
When roll the drums of the foe's advance.
Athos, Porthos, the Musketeers
Ride again in the land of France!

(cont'd., new stanza)

185

Thrust and parry and press the fight!
What of the heroes famed of years?
Lo, they fly with the eagle's flight
When France has need of them — France in tears!
Lo, they laugh at the foreign spears
And sing with the song of guns! Perchance
D'Artagnan and the Musketeers
Ride again in the land of France!

L'ENVOI

Stirrup-cups for the cavaliers,
And the old oath over of old romance —
"One for all!" — and the Musketeers
Ride again in the land of France!

PARIS — 1456

Grim winter stars and goblin moons
Peep through their ragged winding sheet
And many a shadow sweeps and swoons
As Paris dreams and gray wolves meet;
The watch goes by on crunching feet
To halt within yon tavern's light
In envy of its ease and heat —
Villon is drinking deep tonight.

Fair Isabeau beside him croons
A love ballade of haunting beat;
The Abbess broods on yesternoons
When sparrows quarreled among the wheat;
And now a catch roars out to greet
New-beaded stoups or put to flight
The wail of night winds hagged with sleet —
Villon is drinking deep tonight.

(cont'd., new stanza)

Poor beggar of small royal boons,
Cut-purse and drabber, dicer, cheat,
Fellow to sworders, sots, buffoons,
Hunted anon for gallows-meat,
Yet singer of high songs and sweet,
Tender of one grown old and white,
And sooth-sayer for stew and street —
Villon is drinking deep tonight.

L'ENVOI

My lords and gentlemen, we eat,
Toss pots and part from sound and sight.
I wonder in what ingle seat
Villon is drinking deep tonight!

BALLADE OF LADIES OF TIMES GONE BY

(Being yet another translation of Villon's
Ballade des dames du temps jadis.")

Tell me now in what land can be
Flora the Roman? Where remain
Fair Hipparchia's charms and she —
Thais — in beauty so germane?
Echo, calling afar, in vain,
Over the rivers and marshes wan,
Lovelier, once, than girls profane?
But where are the snows of last year gone?

Where's Heloise, that learn'd lady
For whom was gelded — priestly gain! —
Pierre Esbaillart, at Saint Denis?
For love he bore such burden of pain.

(cont'd., no new stanza)

189

And where is the Queen who did ordain
And give command that Buridan
Be sewed in a sack and flung to Seine?
But where are the snows of last year gone?

Queen Blanche, white as a white lily,
Who sang in a voice of siren strain;
Big-foot Berthe, Beatrix, Allys,
And Eremburge who ruled in Maine;
And that good Jeanne, maid of Lorraine,
Burned by the English at Rouen —
Where are they. Virginal Suzerain?
But where are the snows of last year gone?

L'ENVOI

Prince, to ask of this week abstain
Nor seek to learn of this year, anon,
Since will remain the one refrain —
But where are the snows of last year gone?

BALLADE OF LOST ILLUSION

I cannot sing of good Gods, but of great;
Nor think your faiths are stronger than your fears;
Nor say the heron seeks no other mate,
Forgetting and forgot by yesteryear's;
Nor shall I hold that honor more endears
The recreant debtor of his rightful debt;
Nor yet deny, for any lover's ears,
They never shall forgive whose lips have met.

They see and marvel and they name it — fate;
Heart calls to heart across the barriers;
With fumbling fingers they unbar the gate;
They swear vain vows which Heaven never hears.
What reck they now of pillows wet with tears?
Pulses are thunder and flesh flame! And yet
A little knavish whisper flouts and fleers,
"They never shall forgive whose lips have met."

(cont'd., new stanza)

For all love's days and nights are profligate
And all love's ways are wanton till death nears;
And the lone heir of dead desire is hate,
Beggared with kisses, bitter with arrears;
And the soul smarts of little, crafty jeers;
And when appears the shadow of regret
And wisdom, wan with many griefs, appears,
They never shall forgive whose lips have met.

L'ENVOI

Princess and all ye heavy-handed peers,
Learn now this rhyme and nevermore forget —
For life's a wind and love a vane that veers —
They never shall forgive whose lips have met.

BALLADE TO A
LADY IN IDLENESS

The dust of temple and the dust
Of sword and shield and culverin,
The bones of unjust men and just,
Sweet courtezan and pale virgin
Are long as they had never been;
But we forego and we forget
And wonder through the idle din
Why Sappho's lips are singing yet.

We tread in vain our ancient must,
There is no more red wine to win;
Time's table yields no grudging crust,
And faces fair grow pinched and thin.
Say where is now that plenteous inn
Where all the immortal names are met?
Mayhap they have a tale to spin
Why Sappho's lips are singing yet.

(cont'd., new stanza)

Life is a withered mummy thrust
Within a golden palanquin.
Life is a sound of love and lust
Drummed from an empty kilderkin.
Life is a fool that dares begin
To play against an eternal debt.
Life is a cynic asking sin
Why Sappho's lips are singing yet.

L'ENVOI

Ah lady, if the death's head grin
Through veils of rose and mignonette,
Go ask your own low mandolin
Why Sappho's lips are singing yet.

BALLADE OF
ROMANCE DESIRED

Ah, come with me where yet the Rhone
Rolls ever under old Beaucaire;
We two have been to Carcassonne
And found but false enchantments there
And learned how pleasure tires and where
Love dies of kisses, one by one;
Now leave the town, the noise, the glare,
Be Nicolete to Nicolson.

For still the daisy flowers are grown
Not whiter than your insteps bare;
The sentinel that walks alone
Is mute because your face is fair;
Still is it wisdom to beware
A watch upon the walls begun;
And there are lodges green to share;
Be Nicolete to Nicolson.

(cont'd., new stanza)

What gain to kneel at Heaven's throne
Adoring in eternal prayer?
Better a proud desire to own
And into Purgatory fare.
By Godis Holy Heart! I swear
I love not any monk or nun,
But only your sweet hands and hair.
Be Nicolete to Nicolson.

L'ENVOI

Lady, 'tis May but while we care;
With passion's passing all is done;
And after life is death. Ah, dare
Be Nicolete to Nicolson.

RONDEL

Death is only a long forgetting
    After the sundown, hidden away
    In a cool dark bed at the end of day,
While the Gods keep watch and the stars are setting.

Why should we fear to have done with fretting
    At lust and labor and hate and play?
Death is only a long forgetting
    After the sundown, hidden away.

None of us lives without regretting
    The toil we gave for a pauper's pay,
    And we shall be fain at last to say,
What of the weary years and sweating,
"Death is only a long forgetting."

RONDEAU OF REST

Under the hills they dream how Hector bled,
The great old Gods; nor dream that beauty fled
    Out of the earth and hid upon a star
    When Athens ruled no longer. . . . Who shall mar
The changeless, fond illusions of the dead?

And there the gnomes keep fires aglow that shed
A glory on their gold and rubies red . . .
    Who knows what treasures they have hoarded far
                             Under the hills?

And you and I, when all our prayers are said
And we have crept — oh, wearily! — to bed,
    Let us forget the laboring world and bar
    Our sleep against the sound of things that are
And sleep and dream of happier things instead,
                             Under the hills.

SESTINA OF ONE FACE FAIR

I said once in my heart: "Now it is May
   I will put by all bitterness and care
And live a brief while joyously and say
   Mad words of beauty unadorned and bare,
That God shall learn how, even for a day,
   I, too, was young and found my love's face fair."

And seeing how the world was free and fair,
   I went along its roads, as free men may,
Singing mad songs, and all my singing bare
   Such praise of God as only youth can say,
And all my heart was happy without care,
   So much my love's face moved me in that day.

There was a little pool half burned in day,
   Half hidden in deep shadows, and it was fair
With all wild iris and green leaves of May,
   Wherein young girls washed their bright bodies bare;
But while I thought for some sweet word to say
   There came upon me a great pain of care.

(cont'd., new stanza)

For how can man love beauty and yet care
    For one face only more than for a day?
When all God's world is free and all maids fair
    To us who live not well but as we may.
Wherefore we lie along our beds and bare
    Our hearts to bitterness we may not say.

But there is one word I beg leave to say
    Who love not heavy hearts nor any care:
Let God be thanked for madness and for May
    And for a face that is a brief while fair,
Or ever we learn, in some bright hour of day,
    What bitterness there is in love laid bare.

So let it be that when the world is bare
    And we that live can find no heart to say
Great words of God and find no heart to care
    For song, who once went singing through the day,
Yet in some wise there shall be one face fair
    Beyond all dreams we made as all men may.

Have, then, no care for aught beyond your day.
    Though all men say that age is bald and bare,
Life may be fair for one face loved in May.

SESTINA TO A LADY OF STERN VIRTUE

(*After the Provencal of Arnaut Daniel*)

So firm desire hath entered in my heart
    Not any treacherous tearing of the nail
Nor of the beak of shame shall rive apart
    My will to love; and though all men may fail
To beat down scorn with rod or any art,
    I would have joy of thee beyond the pale.

Yet when I think of thee lying proud and pale
    Where no quick man may come, then all my heart
Trembleth and each my fingers to the nail
    Trembleth in fear, so beautiful thou art,
Aye, though thy stern kin's watchfulness must fail —
    So thou wert kind! — to keep our flesh apart.

Why wilt thou hold me in the flesh apart,
    Having met my soul beyond the stablished pale?

(cont'd., no new stanza)

For surely thou know'st well how all my heart
   Crieth for thee and how my members fail
For need of lying near thee where thou art,
   Close as the finger to the constant nail.

Not to another as the flesh the nail
   Hath my soul cleaved, but when we stand apart
Then am I all alone beyond the pale,
   Lost to all use of labor and of art,
And then like any broken branch I fail,
   So great desire hath entered in my heart.

Oh, never yet hath bloomed in any heart
   Since Baron Adam with a blameless nail
Broke skin of fruit, such love as flowers apart,
   Desiring thee across that flaming pale,
Aye, finding Eden only where thou art,
   And where thou art not, finding all things fail.

I shall not fail of Heaven though I fail
   To lie beside thee, for I hang my heart
Upon thee as a cross, aye nail by nail
   Bind it with love forever and, apart,
Not time nor tears nor death come swift and pale
   Shall bar away that vision of love's art.

Go then, my gong, and be a nail in heart
   Of her that lieth where all men part and fail,
Saying to her soul: "In honor's pale thou art!"

RIME-ROYAL OF HIS OWN SINGING

God knows there is no comfort in sad songs
Nor any ease in bitter songs made sweet
With high, wild music of the wind that throngs
Above the thronging walkers in the street
Where men meet men and men and women meet,
Speak of light loves and part and sigh and say,
"Ah, well, 'twill serve to while the hours away!"

For life has many moods and all moods tire
Or ever the cup be drained unto the lees:
Pleasure and song and triumph and desire
And all safe comfort and all wonted ease.
And if a man sit brooding over these
Shall he not hold, of each that bore its day:
"This, too, hath served to while the hours away?"

And if a man sit brooding over grief,
Now, surely, at the last he shall confess

(cont'd., no new stanza)

(Remembering how that every pain was brief
Midmost the limbo of life's barrenness
And how, for every lip that he would press
There lingered yet some savor of decay) —
"All sorrow served to while the hours away."

All beauty has some little dole of death,
All death some hope of beauty hidden there
(Howbeit before the laden west wind's breath
Are blown dead bones that moved in men whilere),
Wherefore we living die not of despair,
But turn and seek such beauty as we may,
Thinking thereof to while the hours away.

So let me sing what songs are in my heart
Before my heart's few singing days are done,
And pardon me if what I can of art
Sound only threnes and dirges 'neath the sun,
Who have but watched how all earth's rivers run
Into a sea that is not filled for aye —
So must I choose to while the hours away.

And, also, now, if any man will read
And muse how there is beauty in sad lays
Beyond all boast of beauty that may breed
In measures made to earn the common praise,
Let me take heart for sadness of my days
And to whatever Gods will hearken, pray
My songs may serve to while some hours away.

RIME-ROYAL OF
BETTER COUNSEL
THAN MOST

Hear in grave silence, but with tongue in cheek,
All moral words of old and godly men;
Hold high your head and be not mean or meek;
If you have coin, go forth and spend it, then;
Desire not as the crowd desires; and when
Passion is dead fear not to go your way
Nor cling to love beyond its pleasant day.

Have not more faith in woman than you must
And not in any man have faith at all;
Remember that his will is ease of lust
And hers but ease of hunger; in your hall
Avoid the pretty poets, great and small,
And learn whereof wise men have said their say;
So shall you, too, be wise in your own day.

Have not to do with lawyers nor with law,
These being dear to merchants and to knaves;

(cont'd., no new stanza)

205

Turn like a lord from quoters of the saw,
"All men are equal, men must not be slaves";
Not always unto harlots go; let graves
Speak of how little time you have to stay
Prouder than worms before your dying day.

That which is well worth learning, learn with ease
In your own chamber far from schoolmen's eyes;
Nor ever teach the ignorant, seeing that these
Are nothing worth forever; in some wise
Hold beauty more than any truth that dies —
All truth being that which any fool may say
To prove how night is only darkened day.

Seek not for happiness, but yet with song
Look life between the brows; and as for death,
Fear not nor hope since, whether weak or strong,
You shall not more endure, for lack of faith,
Than any that has breathed his pious breath
And laid him down and utterly passed away
Beyond remembrance of the passing day.

Lie not, save in such cause as lies began,
And let not falsehood hold your eyes from sleep;
Let never tears rise up for pain of man
And for your own long pain have scorn to weep.
For all things keep a secret jest and keep
A little living doubt of God for aye;
And in the end you shall have lived your day.

HENDECASYLLABICS

All the graves of the Goths the wild world over
Speak for glory and war and love of woman;
All the runes of the Goths and all their folk-lore,
Woven ever with deeds of Thor and Odin,
Echo, gloomy and stern, full of a moaning
Wind in primitive forests, full of thunder
Rolling over stark hills, and boom of ocean
Breaking, older than pain, on broken beaches.

Sad and sodden with drink they watched the winter
Pass and heard in the night the hard wolf-howling,
Saying deep to their spirits: "Lo, the sparrow
Flitteth into a hall and through the torchlight,
Flying but for a moment under rafters,
Then departeth and goeth down the darkness —
So the life of man is come we know not
Whence, and like as a bird is gone forever."

These were berserkers wild in battle, vikings
Ruddy-bearded and bold, blue-eyed and handsome,
Singing songs in the teeth of northern tempests,
Savage, passionate, pagan, meet for sagas.

All the graves of the Goths the wild world over
Speak for glory and war and love of woman.

SAPPHICS I

Slowly dawn came, waking the sleeping Goddess,
Breathing open, even with lips of roses,
Eyes that trembled, half in the dream that held her
                              Yet with Adonis.

Then the young loves harnessed the doves, the wild-
          wing
Doves immortal, bound them with pearl and amber,
Making day ring loud for a sound of movement
                              Sweeter than bird-song.

Out of tired lips fluttered a sigh for waking,
Yet with fingers fitting the purple sandals,
All her bright breast, shaken with stormy kisses,
                              Flashed in the morning.

Then in some wise, like as a mist of April
Passes rainless over the rain-wet meadows,
Borne in wrought gold, wonderful, oh! and laughing,
                              Passed Aphrodite.

(cont'd., new stanza)

All the earth mourned bitterly for that passing,
All the sea sobbed, beaten on lonely beaches,
Yet with deep song, seeing that even heartache
                              Throbbed of her beauty.

But in one place something remained, a fragrance
Laughed and lingered, haunting the windy sunlight,
Aye, a thing man never forgets forever,
                              Once he has known it.

Wherefore, now, let nothing be said against her,
Nay, let no man speak in his heart against her —
Oh Divine One! — seeing that unto Lethe
                              All shall remember.

SAPPHICS II

When with sob-torn throat and with filching fingers
Thou, desirous ever of more and more love,
Lay with crushed breast shuddering and with locked
    arms
                Writhing around me,

Silken-thighed one, beautiful-browed Pyrrinha,
All the night long, over thy form beside me,
Moved a mild air shaken by wings triumphant
                Brooding above us.

Soft are men's mouths honeyed with loves of women,
Strong are men's arms, binding like bands of iron,
Ah, but thy lips, aye and thy slender arms are
                Softer and stronger.

I will bring thee garlands of fairest flowers,
Weave and bring thee delicate blooms and virgin,
All to learn how brighter than all their beauty
                Thou art grown lovely.

(cont'd., new stanza)

Ah, but come now, suffer that I may bathe thee,
Comb thy bound hair burning with combs of amber,
Still with warm wine rousing thy veins, and after
                              I will caress thee.

Curve thy fingers under my breasts and kiss them,
O divine one, bringer of ease in torment!
Rest thy pale brows pillowed upon them, rest thee
                              Pillowed upon them!

ALCAICS

O Wind, O West Wind, singing of Hesperus,
Blow, blow again, now, laden with amaranth,
  Over the place where she lies dreaming,
    Whisper and say to her words I dare not!

Bid her forsake — ah! — bid her forsake for me
Old cold delights long banished by Artemis
  Who, on far Latmus, faint with passion,
    Kisses Endymion's face in secret!

Oh, blow awake, with music aeolian,
Eyes that deny me more than to sing to them!
  Breathe in that mouth desire for comfort
    Sweeter than tears on the mouths of maidens!

Saying, "He loves thee, Sappho!" and saying it
Not as with pride, but tenderly, tenderly
  As of my heart, wherein are only
    Song and the ache of her singing beauty.

Thus, then, it may be she will remember me,
O Wind, O West Wind, sigh and remember me
  When I am gone to fields of Orcus
    Far from the sea and the sun forever!

PART FIVE

Must I recall you only in the rain,
Like men that gather treasures of rich art,
Fondling them over in some room apart
When tired of toil and all things else are vain?

SONNETS OF A MINNESINGER

I

I will have done with following Beauty's face,
Who has no heart of tenderness for me,
But walks alone, mysterious as the sea,
Luring me always from my proper place,
I will have done with all her endless grace,
Since I may not thus follow endlessly,
For I have only seen what all men see
Who cheat death proudly for a little space.
It is as if one, daring before dawn
The keep of some old castle, thinks to find
Something of triumph, having left behind
Dark muttering halls where nameless ghosts have trod,
But suddenly through the roof looks out upon
The impregnable bright battlements of God.

(cont'd., new stanza)

215

II

When my heart breaks at last with beauty of sound
Gone always, like some elfin violin,
Beyond full hearing, weird and sweet and thin
And never to be caught up and never found,
Oh, bury me then so deep down in the ground
That I shall hear no music more of sin
Or burning of red clouds when dawns begin
Or ever again hear faint, far bugles wound.
And bury me where the wind has all forgot
To whisper of still moons at midnight, where
No breeze may wanton through a woman's hair,
And surely where no ribald gales conspire
To boast how sails crept home to Camelot
And purple sails bore boldly forth from Tyre.

(cont'd., new stanza)

III

If sonnets and if songs were made for this —
To burn upon love's altars and to stay,
Even for the passing of an autumn day,
Oblivion from the memory of a kiss —
They had been dumb beneath the Acropolis
And we had never heard one roundelay
Of Ermengarde's or Borgia's beauty — nay,
Nor what wild passion flamed in Tomyris.
But one who sits in silence and apart,
Maddened with bitter melodies and sweet,
Shall rise and wander singing through the street,
Heedless of hindrance in the mocking throngs,
And pluck the broken lutestrings of his heart
For sonnets and for little sounding songs.

(cont'd., new stanza)

IV

Yet if wise men smile down at you and say:
"Ah, well, but you are young and some few years
Will etch your face with acid of such tears
As only age can wholly dry away" —
Let not these ancients rob you of your day,
Who are themselves half mad with grisly fears
Of one that hath not eyes nor nose nor ears
Nor any soft warm fingers fit for play.
The old are bitter for lost youth; the old
Shiver in rags of worn philosophies;
They are dying from life; the very words of these
Smack of dead bones and blasted ecstasy;
But O thou youth of the roses and the gold,
Ride hard, love long, drink deep, live dangerously!

(cont'd., new stanza)

V

Last year I loved a lady — oh, as fair
As ever queen that men have bled to kiss,
And now my whole heart's chalice, poured with bliss,
Brims in the fragrance of your hands and hair.
I cannot dream of loving otherwhere
Than your soft indolence of beauty is,
Yet all the dead past haunts me, whispering this:
"Next year thou shalt remember, but not care."
I think there is no bitterer wine to sup
Than when man's idols have been tumbled down
He needs must grave new images and crown
New Gods in ancient temples. Oh, as gall
And utter wormwood in a golden cup,
Not whom we love, but love, is all in all.

(cont'd., new stanza)

VI

Not with wild words nor yet with wilder tears
Can we two kiss and part, for we have taken
Fame for our God and finally have forsaken
Love and all faiths of love and all love's fears.
Oh, we of the singing lips, we have stopped our ears
And left forever the hearth-side; we are shaken
Far too deep down with dawn winds to awaken
And go about the business of love's years.
Yet for a bright, brief while let us pretend
That our two hearts hold passion overmuch,
Sweet to the taste and sweeter to the touch
And flown with madness and all mirth whereof
The great Gods yield a little, before the end
For the sound and glory and ruffling drums of love.

(cont'd., new stanza)

VII

A strange thing happened only yesterday,
For when I saw you walking in the sun
I half forgot you were a skeleton,
So gracefully I marked you swing and sway,
And, somehow gloriously, were veiled away
The barren bones and you appeared as one
Carved out of flame or as a spirit spun
On God's own loom to make an angel gay.
Ah, well, it was a trick of thought, a jest
Played by the beast within me which knows not
That all its days, since ever 'twas begot,
Bulk not so large as one drop in the sea,
But, looking on the movement of your breast,
Sings as the Sons of God might — passionately.

(cont'd., new stanza)

VIII

You beauty, oh, you beauty! Paint your eyes
And paint your cheeks and lips and bring desire
Leaping along my veins to be the sire
Of little death's-heads like us in some wise.
Fool me with kisses and with enterprise
Delude me till I tremble like a wire
Plucked by a poet's fingers at a lyre
Deep among roses when the winter dies.
Your flesh is thinner than a comet's tail,
Your bones alone are matter; and I would
There were more color in your fevered blood
To hide the empty arches of your hips.
Ah, love, why must you be so always pale?
Paint and yet paint your eyes and cheeks and lips!

(cont'd., new stanza)

IX

Yet if I get a child from you, I think
I must go forth and laugh whole hours away,
Remembering how two skeletons at play
Forged out a third and made the high Gods blink.
Oh, I must call for company and drink
Deeper than ever sage or satyr may
And mark upon a calendar and say,
"Thus to the chain of death, another link!"
How dead men's bones do breed and multiply,
As if they are informed with force and dream,
That three-score years and ten of sentient gleam
Between two nothings make a living thing.
And — O my dear — as if this you and I
Can really lust and love and sob and sing.

(cont'd., new stanza)

X

What have we learned and still what can we learn
More than they knew who pictured in dim caves
The hunting of the aurochs by young braves
And the going forth to war and the return?
What do we know more than our eyes discern
And our hands touch? And that sound comes in waves?
And how strewn flowers are fragrant on new graves?
And on the lips how bitterly tears burn?
Ah love, let men fling plummets down the sky
Beyond the radiance of the farthest star
And etch on ultimate atom-points the scar
Of their insatiate science. By and by
They may learn all there is of how. But why —
Ah, there's the test! Why are things what they are?

(cont'd., new stanza)

XI

Serene in God's high gardens, do they stand
And look beyond the stars to this dim earth,
Smiling, it may be, in reflective mirth,
The old kings hard of justice and of hand?
Do they regret the war-axe and the brand
That hewed out hearts for pastime of great birth
In days when all things else were little worth
And proud men jousted at a maid's command?
I think that they sit even as did Canute
When bidding the serried stallions of the sea
Break from their charge and fawn subserviently
To vindicate a fop's wild impudence —
That those old warriors watch, amazed and mute,
The vanity of the world's intelligence.

(cont'd., new stanza)

XII

When you sit naked at your looking-glass,
Having combed hair, with kisses in your eyes,
Where the gold light falls intimately and lies
Tingeing your limbs to color of bright brass,
And when you see how silken movements pass
Through slender breasts and delicate flesh of thighs
And being proud for beauty and most wise
In all love's ways and wizardries alas! —
I wonder do you sometimes muse the while
And feel a sudden tenderness for men
Denied the solace of your body then
When their lips left you passionless and cool?
Or do you watch but your own grace and smile
As once Narcissus down a sylvan pool?

(cont'd., new stanza)

XIII

I think of you as I must think of one
Standing beneath a sail when toward the west
Bore forth some Norseman to a far conquest
While the sharp spray went hissing in the sun,
Singing of heroes till the race was run
And the long oars were silent and at rest
And tired men sought the beauty of her breast
And the deep horns went round when day was done.
I think of you gone laughing to the breath
Of great waves crashed among the painted shields,
Your hair blown out like flame of ravished fields
In conquered lands, and in your heart a fire
Wilder than war and dangerous more than death
And hard and haughty and bright past all desire.

(cont'd., new stanza)

XIV

You that have mystery, you that have dark hair,
Smooth arms to kiss and small breasts and long hips,
You that delight, with sensitive fingertips,
To touch warm gold and soft warm flesh and fair,
O you of the bitter eyes and the tired air
Of Sappho singing low through sobbing lips
Bruised for being crushed all night by one who sips
Delectably rich wines of pleasure there —
Although you are a singer and care less
For any man or me or any thing
Than only that God give you days to sing
The banners in your blood out, passionately,
Sometimes desire shall lend you tenderness
Deep in the night when you remember me.

(cont'd., new stanza)

XV

Some day, when time has left you calm and wise
To look at last within your glass and say,
"Can it be true that sober men and gay
Loved this face, once, and kissed these weary eyes?
That there was ever aught in the replies
These old and writhen lips could once betray
To heal and hurt the passion of a day
Or in cold hands the touch that pacifies?" —
Will you remember, being heartsick, then,
That, woven in some little song of mine
Your name for warp made all the woof's design
Brilliant and beautiful and like to shed
Something of pride hereafter among men?
Will you remember and be comforted?

(cont'd., new stanza)

XVI

Next year when it is winter out of doors,
You'll sit and read some old-world writer's book,
Marvelling briefly on the pains he took
And wondering idly why the chimney roars;
And where the firelight flickers on the floors
You'll say that it is sunlight on a brook;
And so, secure within your ingle nook,
Sip cider and munch apples to their cores.
And you'll not heed the wind against the walls
Nor hear your name being bandied by the wind.
Why should you sigh for any ghost that sinned
And loved your face a little and is dead?
But you will start awake when your book falls,
And rise and yawn and seek your warm dark bed.

(cont'd., new stanza)

XVII

When you are come to three-score years and ten
If, nodding in your chair, you dream on me
And wake to smile a little, wearily,
Thinking, "For he was like as other men,"
I shall have been long dead, long buried, then
(Haply beside some ever-sounding sea),
But should you muse and sigh regretfully,
"He came and kissed and never came again" —
Then think how, on the very lips of love,
The serpents' tongues we seek to kiss away
Grow ever sharp and deadlier, day by day,
Even as hearts grow older, aye, and old,
And think how better is the loss thereof
Than tenderness turned bitter and touch cold.

(cont'd., new stanza)

XVIII

And yet I think that when you lie by night
Quietly there beside him who, asleep,
Dreams of his goods — that you will sometimes weep
For me within whose arms you drank delight.
Not to the valley but the windy height,
Not to the shore but driving down the deep
You might have gone with me — and you will keep
Something of hurt to plague you, fierce and bright.
Seeker of peace, have comfort! Death will come
Decently some day, with the neighbors in
And one to shrive you clean of what small sin
Clings to your placid soul. Nor need you tell
How in the distance throbs a riotous drum
And through the gathering darkness peals a bell.

(cont'd., new stanza)

XIX

I shall remember you, I shall recall
The spray-wet wind upon your tumbled hair,
And wonder what you look like, rocking there
Among your slender girls, your boys grown tall,
And wonder if you think, wrapped in your shawl,
Of how I loved your face when it was fair
Beyond all grace that other women wear
Forever and forever and for all.
Oh, "Yet a little sleep, a little slumber,
A little folding of the hands to sleep"?
But now it is a brave thing, clean and deep,
And there is in you something gleaming, now,
With no dull days forgotten save by number
And no long pondering over why and how.

(cont'd., new stanza)

XX

Must I recall you only in the rain,
Like men that gather treasures of rich art,
Fondling them over in some room apart
When tired of toil and all things else are vain?
Must I desire you only when old pain
Will leave me sometimes happy and my heart
Tingles with hunger for the swift new smart
Love blows along the senses to the brain?
Never! But I will keep you as men keep
Some vision of life's meaning in the night
Or follow by day some purpose of delight
Beckoning them and beckoning them, until
All dreams are lost in that foregathering sleep
Where there's no love left and all songs are still.

(cont'd., new stanza)

XXI

If we had met and parted in such wise
As tall ships meet and part upon the sea —
Speak word of ports and pass irrevocably,
Each to its haven under different skies —
If, with calm hands and eyes on radiant eyes,
With laughing lips and hearts from anguish free,
We two had kissed and parted joyously,
Turning with never tears away, nor sighs —
Ah, love, I had remembered all my days
And it had been, with all life overpassed,
Had heard you singing somewhere at the last,
Serene beyond the Pleiads, where the shore
Beats to a paean wrung from lonely ways:
"Whom the Gods join are sealed forevermore!"

(cont'd., new stanza)

XXII

Not to great music nor from lips ablaze
With passion of singing songs flown out like fire,
These verses, fashioned to a broken lyre
In somber cities and forgotten ways,
Have little of April's madness or of May's
And little of June's intolerable desire,
They do not ache with August nor suspire
In purple and amber wrung from autumn days.
I am no singer such as others are
Whose throats are gold bells pealing over the land;
They are the bards of nations and they stand
In kings' halls, clothed in velvet and in vair;
While I but murmur, at a casement bar,
Idylls and threnes, because your face is fair.

(cont'd., new stanza)

XXIII

Since all love's ways and all love's wounds are sweet
And there's not any bitterness in love,
Let us forget the utter end thereof,
Trodden down swiftly by remorseless feet,
And let us stand with arms flung wide to greet
The broken body of the dying dove
With not more wisdom than we gaze above
And dream God reigns forever. Ah, repeat
No more the bitter songs that I have made
Nor more the sounding sonnets. If to us
This ringing day has entered glorious,
Why should we dread the sunset? Shall the bars
Of night be closer or more firmly stayed?
Dawn is a veil drawn down to hide the stars.

NAPOLEON

Thy name is bright with sabers and thy name
Is big with guns; magnificent and stern
The somber eagles brood above thine urn
Between the moldering standards' dusty flame;
And still across the empires men acclaim
The splendor of thy destiny and turn
Still to thy terrible battle fires that burn
In distant, billowing holocausts of fame.
O thou proud Lucifer, thou Morning Star,
Thou brilliant, cold, white glory in the West,
The heart's drums thunder, breaking in the breast,
For muttering o'er thy triumphs, one by one,
As if again were bugles blown for war
Through streets gone brave with banners in the sun!

TO A POET DYING YOUNG

You came and there was music, for your hands
Swept suddenly from dusty, slumbering strings
A rapture as of half-remembered things,
A glory of dim days and ancient lands,
And something valiant as of broken brands
And clean and swift as of a lark that sings
Joyously under heaven on young wings,
And something sad, too, as of drifted sands.
You came and there was music. And for us
There never shall be throbbing viols again
Without the sense of something gone from men,
Something of beauty vanished from the hill
Whereon you walked a brief while glorious.
The rest is silence. But the stars are still!

VIKINGS

So all day long they rowed, and with a song
Wilder than wings of gulls, Leif Ericsson
Stood to the tiller, calling, one by one
Great praise on Gods and heroes; all night long
Bellowed the waves with thunder; bold and strong
The thews of Thor bore to the sunken sun,
Heavy in hammered gold, until they won
Through Ymir's blood and winds that brawl and throng.
Ha! Not from these the darkness of the deep
Struck terror, nor the tempest; not from these
The Spaniard's prayer for sweet familiar seas,
Blown warm with summer scents, wherein to lave,
But only, after labor, the sad sleep
And the bright name and glory of the brave.

BORGIA

No more the furious revels and no more
The dangerous trysts and secret nights of love
Nor any more forever the songs whereof
The halls of Rome were amorous of yore.
Now is that palace unto ruin given o'er,
The walls grown loathsome with soft things that move,
And owls have refuge in the roofs above
And asps and adders and scorpions on the floor.
I dreamed of thee again, last night, and stood
Against the curtains of thy tumbled bed,
Seeing the fallen hair about thine head
And all the broken beauty that was thine,
And seeing upon thy mouth a trace of blood
And under thee crushed roses and spilt wine.

IN MEMORIAM

I would arise now, since none other sings
The beauty and the glory that are gone,
I would arise and utter a song, drawn
Forth of long brooding over muted strings.
For late I dreamed one came on splendid wings,
Between the dusks of sunset and of dawn,
Wherefrom a feather brushed my lips upon,
Sealing them unto silence for base things,
And clear and sweet as one great chord vibrates
Beyond its full concordances of sound,
There rang a voice in all the air around,
Bell-toned, like surf upon reverberant shores.
Crying: "Lift up, lift up your heads, O Gates,
Be ye lift up, ye everlasting doors!"

OLD MAID

God knows how many nights upon her bed
She dreamed another Latmus, while the hot
Sweet winds of summer in her garden plot
Kissed away tears from roses comforted.
God knows what flaming verses she has read
To keep vicarious trysts with Lancelot,
Broken with brooding over loves forgot
And lawless revels of the pagan dead.
But she has conquered all her blood's desire,
Cheated her soul of sin as misers cheat,
And now she pauses on proud, hesitant feet
At lighted rooms where men and women mix,
With amorous eyes fearful of unknown fire —
A naked nun clasping the crucifix!

THE JEST

Phaon, when Aphrodite made you over,
Gave you bright youth and beauty and dark hair
And touched your flesh and left it firm and fair
To eat thick honey and lie all day in clover,
She fetched from Heaven a wondrous cloak to cover
Your shoulders broad with boat labor, and there
Robed you in princely raiment, made you heir
To lips of her who had been Athis' lover.
All these good gifts the Goddess gave you, Phaon,
But, as I think, she must have left you blind,
Seeing that you walk in Lesbian ways nor find
Those little fragrant foot-prints on the shore.
Gods! What a sorry jest was this to play on
One who had else been dead forevermore!

TO OMAR KHAYYAM

Persian! I fill with red, forbidden wine
This cup grown dusty from long abstinence
And pledge that leisure when, for recompense,
On some green garden's bank I shall recline,
Listing your praise of beauty and the vine
And scorn of little men's intelligence
And pity of it and of that insolence
Which must have right and wrong in things divine.
For there are many blown so big with pride
They think they wear God's likeness! And they think
God cares a single cent though all men drink
To drown a little sorrow from their days,
Who are but vermin dreaming they shall ride
On deathless wings through infinite times and ways!

CONRAD

Grey gulls now and a grey sea feigning sleep;
Grime on the barren decks at the river's mouth;
And old men sitting in taverns as if loath
Either to face a gale or to lie and weep.
Only the old men now, and the gulls may sweep
Over inscrutable oceans — ah, but an oath
Suddenly rings far out of the sullen south
And winds throng out of the distance, full and deep.
Sailor of ships, ahoy! You pass in the light
Bound for a port beyond the roads of men.
We are not like to speak your soul again,
Time is too wide. You loom beneath your spars,
Crowding on sail and standing toward the night
Across the infinite oceans of the stars!

BOSWORTH FIELD

The sound of swords, the shock of broken shields
Rang in a fury of war that has been here
Where now the notes of noon serene and clear,
Call home the tillers of these little fields.
Here raged Plantagenet, like a king that wields
Doom of an ax foredoomed before the spear
Of some king chosen by the Gods to fear
Death nor defeat nor any flesh that yields.
Almost again I see the dust clouds there,
Thronged on a wind above their heavy horse,
Smell the bright carnage reddening round his corse
Who fell forever with the fallen Rose
And hear again that turbulent music where,
Thundered of drums, the Tudor's triumph goes.

ACROSTIC

If this poor sonnet should be found some day
In a book long forgotten of other men,
I wonder if his wit will spell out, then,
What secret lies within it, hidden away,
Who, in old hours of night, may seek to say
Some word concerning us and bring again
Our wit within the pale of the world's ken
For gain or pride or pleasure — Sir, I pray
That if you muse upon it and retrace
The long and weary effort of a name
To leave some letter on the wall of fame,
Oh, muse in such wise as the good God must!
Damn not, I pray you for Our Lady's grace,
Nor smile, remembering how I am but dust!

J. U. Nicolson
"The King of the Black Isles"

J. U. Nicolson (1885-1944) was a twentieth-century American poet and translator of poetry. Born John Urban Nicolson, he spent most of his professional life in Chicago, Illinois where he worked as a ware-house manager. Nicolson first achieved notice as a "column poet," so-called for the appearance of his early work in the literary columns of several Chicago newspapers under the pseudonym, "The King of the Black Isles." In addition to his own writings, J. U. Nicolson is remembered for his rendering into modern English of *The Canterbury Tales* of Geoffrey Chaucer.